The Forward Book of Poetry

2021

This anthology was designed and produced by Bookmark, the sponsor of the Forward Prizes. Bookmark is a global content and communications company based in London, Toronto, Montreal, Santiago, Lima, New York, LA, Shanghai and Singapore. Bookmark uses consumer insights to develop compelling content for brands that engages consumers and drives sales. Clients include Patek Philippe, Air Canada, HSBC, LATAM, Bombardier, Explora, Aberdeen Standard, Fidelity, American Express Travel, Silhouette, Hudson Yards, Pandora and StreetSmart. bookmarkcontent.com @bookmarkcontent

The Forward Book of Poetry

BOOKM/RK

LONDON

First published in Great Britain by
Bookmark · 1 St John's Lane · London ECIM 4BL
in association with
Faber & Faber · Bloomsbury House · 74-77 Great Russell Street
London WCIB 3DA

ISBN 978 0 571 36248 6 (paperback)

Printed and bound by CPI Group (UK) · Croydon CRO 4YY

A CIP catalogue reference for this book
is available at the British Library.

To Roddy Lumsden, in memoriam

Contents

The Forward Prize for Best Collection
    Selected poems from the shortlisted books

The Felix Dennis Prize for Best First Collection
    Selected poems from the shortlisted books

The Forward Prize for Best Single Poem
    Shortlisted poems

Highly Commended Poems 2020

Foreword

Many longstanding cultural events have fallen by the wayside in 2020 and are very much missed. But the *Forward Book of Poetry* has not been cancelled or postponed. Publishers managed to send in their books and the Forward Foundation team kept us all on track. In different corners of the country, five judges – Leaf Arbuthnot, Kim Moore, Roger Robinson, David Wheatley and myself – sat reading as the world changed. We read on a grand scale: 208 full collections and 205 single poems. Though we had to meet on our computer screens rather than in person, it was an honour to chair the careful, generous debates that resulted in our shortlists. There were comments so astute I'll remember them always, and I could have carried on listening all week. Now, happily, the annual anthology is here to celebrate some of the most exciting new work in international poetry and to suggest the great variety of what is being published right now in Great Britain and Ireland.

The period of our judging coincided almost exactly with the first two months of lockdown in the UK. None of the books in our hands were written for a pandemic, and prophecy certainly wasn't among our criteria, but it was noticeable how often a strong poem would seem as true to the hour and the day as the constantly updated news. Poems of touch, of distance, of silence; of microscopy, of neighbourliness, of nature's resilience: all reached out into the present. Poets specialise in making wholes of incongruous parts; they know how the ordinary can lap against the astounding; how time can shrink and stretch.

I was particularly struck by questions of scale. Opening some collections, a great blast of choric power was immediately palpable; crowds and continents rose into view, voices sounded in my lone mind as if in a stadium. Elsewhere, there were people talking quietly, not assuming any company, attending perhaps to a singular recollection or the merest shiver of wind through grass. I'm sure the conditions of reading made me acutely aware of this, confined to home as I was, except for a daily excursion to the neighbourhood meadow. I was paying attention to small shifts in the view from my window and following the unfolding drama of new chestnut leaves, adapting to a radically contracted geography while awaiting updates on a shared situation that was affecting all humankind. A microbe too small to see was causing global changes visible from space. What is large? What is small? How can we think carefully, as we must, on many different scales? Poetry has been working at such quandaries for millennia, weighing epic and lyric, strength-testing pastoral, pivoting from a wide panorama to an egg or a bee-hive or a single hand outstretched.

It was a bit extreme to read two hundred books from a single year, but almost everyone, it seemed, wanted a poem of some sort in spring 2020. Journalists were reading their choices on the radio, shopkeepers were posting them in shuttered windows. On my street, we started to read poems together from our doorways; we tried prose but it wouldn't do. 'Poetry is having a moment' announced *Vanity Fair*. Poetry had a moment that lasted through both world wars. It has a moment whenever there is pressure and threat, and whenever we want to think carefully – together or individually. In times of distraction it can carve out a space of concentration. Poems can shake or shock or magnetise our ideas into new configurations. Poems can offer complex forms of consolation – for example in suggesting a pattern where there seemed only disconnected shards – but we might also value them for being tough and refusing to soothe us, or for taking no notice of us at all and remaining intent on purposes of their own.

Among the poems featured here from shortlisted collections you'll find the yellow blaze of a broom bush lighting an intriguingly stocked mental larder; the tiger ferocity of a grandmother; a vertiginous descent down a woman's throat; the relics of a gypsy life vanishing in silence. You'll find the rhythmic sway of lovers in a gleaming, athletically agile lyric that is, so far as I know, for all the centuries of love poetry, like nothing written before.

All of which I hope suggests the glorious particularity of these poems, their capacity to surprise, the push and pull between strangeness and familiarity, the impossibility of summing up. Even so, there are striking recurrences. Many of the shortlisted books draw into their rich weave at least one language other than English, and explore the hybrid forms that emerge. We find names 'writ in bahasa', as Will Harris in *RENDANG* borrows from Keats but lets the water, this time, ripple with Indonesian words. Nina Mingya Powles starts to dream in Chinese characters and crafts delicate, glinting elegies from among the repetitions and disjunctions of language learning. Elsewhere, English meets Romani, and Mojave, and Spanish. Six hundred years ago Chaucer skeined Norman with English, glossing words when he thought we might not understand them; the language has never rested since. Today's linguistic meetings are rarely philological fireworks let off for effect but intimate, improvisatory encounters, or questing sorties into family history.

These poets find form for the experience of inhabiting multiple places, holding together different kinds of life. Martha Sprackland's *Citadel* articulates an extraordinary kinship and doubling across time with a sixteenth-century Spanish queen; Ella Frears thinks with Barbara Hepworth and is haunted by Joan of Arc. With wit and style and mercurial quickness, Rachel Long considers the questions raised by her mother's hair and imagines the hair of a future son. There are terrifically bold, fearless poems of seduction here. And many other kinds of desire surge in besides: desire to argue and experiment, to write, to work. *I Want! I Want!* Vicki Feaver titles her collection. Is it a shout or a whisper? Is that a little girl or a pensioner setting up the ladder and reaching for the moon? There is electric writing about age. Childhood may be separated from later life by little more than a comma; a grandmother's Welsh greenhouse might hold a jungle and another continent, within it.

Beyond the shortlists, there's a generous selection of commended poems, each deeply loved by one or more judge, and pointing towards a whole body of work by an admired writer. All of us – even the most seasoned poetry readers – made discoveries. For my part, I was interested in the unexpected wealth of religious poetry, and the transformation of Christianity's art forms – psalms, canticles, prayers – for secular expression. I was drawn to poetry of meditative watchfulness, but also to boldness and high velocity. It was a joy to find demanding poetic forms employed with superb craftsmanship: haibuns balancing discursive prose on slender haikus; sestinas steadily ringing out their ritual changes.

Many of the books represented here arrived in the world – after years of work – without the celebrations that would usually have greeted them. Gone were the launch parties and reassuring toasts, the pub gigs, the festival marquees. Gone were the tables in bookshops piled with just-published delights to waylay the shopper en route to Crime or Cookery. Dark were the public libraries with their lovely carousels of new titles by the seats and the photocopier. Superb events sprang up online, and many booksellers worked tirelessly to fulfil orders, but it was, and it remains, a difficult time for publishing. For those who like to sit and browse, perhaps this selection might be a New Books Table in compact form. Certainly we hope it will be an invitation to read more. Whatever most attracts you, please raise a glass and bid it welcome.

Alexandra Harris
Chair of the judges
May 2020

Preface

The Forward Prizes for Poetry are more like a series of provocations than a set of monuments. The poets honoured over the years are not placed on plinths. Instead, they become points of reference in a thousand different conversations, and – sometimes – they shape the big C Conversation in a way that few at the time could have foreseen.

Just five years ago, in 2015, *Citizen* by Claudia Rankine won the Forward Prize for Best Collection. Its most striking page names black men whose murders have made waves in the USA since 2012. With each reprint the list grows longer, but the words opposite stay the same:

because white men can't
police their imagination
black men are dying

In this graveyard context, the word 'imagination' startles. Far from make-believe and play, here it is the force that cocks the trigger and makes corpses of the young. Yet how can a poet, a dealer in imagination, call for its policing?

Rankine was issuing both a warning and an invitation. The stories we hear, share and tell are not innocent: they shape the ways that people trust and fear. Songs, novels, films, plays and poems all train us. We can sit dutifully and be schooled by them, bowing down in homage to established canons, or we can answer back, start up a conversation, see where that takes us.

The poems shortlisted and highly commended for the Forward Prizes certainly incite – and highlight – conversation. The Best Collection shortlist alone has as many dramas as Netflix, once you know how to spot them. The speaker in Vicki Feaver's poem '1974' responds to a dull party question 'What do you do?' with a fib that becomes triumphant truth – '"I'm a poet!" I lied / jolting myself to life' – while the voices in the work of David Morley, Natalie Diaz and Pascale Petit speak languages that re-tune the senses, to the unsaid and the silenced.

When a Caroline Bird poem features an angel with a feedback form 'asking how I'd rate my life (very good, good, average, bad, very bad)', how many readers have the discipline to read on without asking themselves the same? The response, each time, is part of the poem.

I thought of this when reading the question-and-answer interviews with this year's 15 shortlisted poets, which we share on our website. From California, Natalie Diaz turned the tables on what she called 'the Forward Prize family, meaning all of you who help to make it happen'.

> I was taught that language is an energy that began long before me but that was moving through me… You do a similar work with this prize, with the community of readers it creates. I wonder… how does being part of this energetic stream of poetry lead you into your hours, days, and lives? I imagine it changes you as much as it changes those who are awarded the prize.

Her question continues to ripple through the Forward Arts Foundation, the charity responsible for the Forward Prizes and for National Poetry Day. If we are, as Diaz says, a 'family' then the family is far bigger than our board, staff team and volunteers: it includes all who have been included in a Forward book of poetry, submitted poems, attended our events or browsed our website. It includes the 'community of readers', as well as those who identify as 'writers' – for all writers are readers first. It includes all who support our work promoting knowledge and enjoyment of poetry.

You can find some of our responses to Diaz on the Foundation's website: they include poet David Wheatley's awareness, as a 2020 judge, that 'in reading it is often poetry that judges me… [it] addresses me with an energy I must match before there can be dialogue'.

There it is, again – the possibility of dialogue, of answering back. In normal years, the audience at the Forward Prizes ceremony has the chance to express what it feels about the poets on stage with live applause and turbo-charged bar-side discussion. This year, Covid-19 rules out a mass gathering, but more spaces for conversation have opened up. For the first time, we have invited the public to a series of Forward Meet The Poet online events: it will make this year's selection of poetry accessible to many more than we ever crammed into Southbank Centre's hospitable halls.

We have long awarded prizes to students who write the best poetry responses to the Forward Prizes shortlist, in partnership with the English and Media Centre, organisers of the Forward/emagazine Creative Critics competition. This year, we have gone one further by e-publishing *From Poem to Poem*, a handbook by Kate Clanchy, teacher and poet, that shows how 12 recent Forward-shortlisted poems can kickstart students into extraordinary writing, featuring the work of teenage poets inspired by Ella Frears, Vicki Feaver, David Morley, Raymond Antrobus, Mary Jean Chan and others. It is a must-read, not just for teachers and students but for all who sense that conversations about a poem are never just conversations about a poem. Please buy it through our website.

The Forward Prizes rely on the careful reading and thoughtful consideration of their judges. As spring 2020 progressed, Covid-19 lockdowns shut schools and nurseries, and impacted livelihoods. Our judges found themselves in very different circumstances than they may have imagined when they first agreed to read the 205 collections and 208 single poems. Our thanks go to our chair – writer, critic and social historian Alexandra Harris – to poets Kim Moore, Roger Robinson and David Wheatley, and to journalist Leaf Arbuthnot, for their unstinting dedication and care.

Thank you, too, Casey Jones, Robin Castle, Alex Courtley, Lucy Coles and Simon Hobbs and everyone at our sponsors, Bookmark – the content marketing agency formerly known as Forward Worldwide. Bookmark has supported us from the very start: their commitment over the past 29 years is an example to all in literary sponsorship. As well as supporting the prizes, the staff at Bookmark work long hours with great skill to make this book.

We are grateful to Arts Council England, to the estate of the late Felix Dennis – which supports the Felix Dennis Prize for Best First Collection – and to the Esmée Fairbairn Foundation and the John Ellerman Foundation. Thank you, too, to fellow trustees of the Forward Arts Foundation, Martin Thomas, Giles Spackman, Bidisha, Kim Evans and Jamie Andrews.

Thanks to the Foundation's staff, particularly to Holly Hopkins, the Forward Prizes manager, for dealing so deftly with all the changes this year threw at her – including the challenge of making the prizes digital at short notice – to Natalie Charles for her design eye, and to Susannah Herbert, the executive director, who continues to ensure these prizes grow in importance year on year. Emily Hasler, John Clegg and Rachel Piercey have been intimately involved in the making of the book, ensuring the poets and their poems are represented properly. The cover is the work of Ness Wood.

William Sieghart
Founder of the Forward Prizes for Poetry
June 2020

Shortlisted Poems
The Forward Prize for Best Collection

Caroline Bird

Dive Bar

Through a red door down a steep flight
of stairs into a windowless cellar
with sweating walls
an ingénue in a smoking jacket
sits atop a piano
as a host of swaying women
sing 'Your Secret's Safe with Me'
and one invites you
into the privacy of a kiss – all these
dark clandestine places – and you find
yourself imagining a very tiny
woman walking straight
into her mouth
through a red door down a steep flight
of throat into a windowless cell
with breathing walls
an ingénue in a smoke jacket
sits astride a piano
as a host of swallowed women
sing 'Your Secret's in a Safe',
the barmaid shakes a custom
cocktail she calls 'A Private Kiss' – all these
dark half-eaten faces – and you find
yourself imagining a tiny tiny
woman walking straight
into her mouth
through a red breath down a dark
thought into a swallowed sense
with shrinking walls
an innuendo in stomach acid
slops upon a piano
as a host of silent passions
mouth 'Your Secret is Yourself'

inside the belly of the world – all these
dark dissolving spaces – and you find
yourself imagining a windowless
woman breaking
walls down in herself, sprinting
up the shrinking
halls and up contracting
corridors and up the choking
fits of hard stares through dark
thoughts and dead
laws through the red door
as it swallows shut behind you
now you're spat out
on the pavement with
the sun just
coming out.

Rookie

You thought you could ride a bicycle
but, turns out, those weren't bikes
they were extremely bony horses. And that wasn't
a meal you cooked, that was a microwaved
hockey puck. And that wasn't a book that was
a taco stuffed with daisies. What if
you thought you could tie your laces?
But all this time you were just wrapping
a whole roll of sellotape round your shoe and
hoping for the best? And that piece of paper
you thought was your tax return?
A crayon drawing of a cat. And your best friend
is actually a scarecrow you stole from a field
and carted away in a wheelbarrow.
Your mobile phone is a strip of bark
with numbers scratched into it.
Thousands of people have had to replace
their doors, at much expense, after you
battered theirs to bits with a hammer
believing that was the correct way
to enter a room. You've been pouring pints
over your head. Playing card games with a pack
of stones. Everyone's been so confused
by you: opening a bottle of wine with a cutlass,
lying on the floor of buses, talking to
babies in a terrifyingly loud voice.
All the while nodding to yourself like
'Yeah, this is how it's done.'
Planting daffodils in a bucket of milk.

Natalie Diaz

Blood-Light

My brother has a knife in his hand.
He has decided to stab my father.

This could be a story from the Bible,
if it wasn't already a story about stars.

I weep alacranes—the scorpions clatter
to the floor like yellow metallic scissors.

They land upside down on their backs and eyes,
but writhe and flip to their segmented bellies.

My brother has forgotten to wear shoes again.
My scorpions circle him, whip at his heels.

In them is what stings in me—
it brings my brother to the ground.

He rises, still holding the knife.
My father ran out of the house,

down the street, crying like a lamplighter—
but nobody turned their lights on. It is dark.

The only light left is in the scorpions—
there is a small light left in the knife too.

My brother now wants to give me the knife.
Some might say, *My brother wants to stab me.*

He tries to pass it to me—like it is a good thing.
Like, *Don't you want a little light in your belly?*

Like the way Orion and Scorpius—
across all that black night—pass the sun.

My brother loosens his mouth—
between his teeth, throbbing red Antares.

One way to open a body to the stars, with a knife.
One way to love a sister, help her bleed light.

Waist and Sway

I never meant to break—

but streetlights dressed her gold.
The curve and curve of her shoulders—
the hum and hive of them,
moonglossed pillory of them—
nearly felled me to my knees.

How can I tell you—the amber of her.
The body of honey—I took it in my hands.

Oh, City—where hands turned holy—

her city, where my hands went undone—
gone to ravel, to silhouette, to moths at the mercy
of the pale of her hips. Hips that in the early night
to light lit up—to shining sweet electricus,
to luminous and lamp—where ached to drink
I did till drunk.

Where in her rocked the dark Zikmund—
her, by then, a cathedral tower.
One breast, rose window.
One breast, room of alchemists.
Where from her came a tolling—
the music of yoke and crown,
of waist and sway.

Wanting her was so close to prayer—
I should not. But it was July,
and in a city where desire means, *Upstairs
we can break each other open*,
the single blessing I had to give was *Mouth*—
so gave and gave I did.

Every night has a woman for temptation.
Every city has a fable for fruit—
like in the castle gardens, where jackdaws waited
glaze-eyed along the walls for a taste of new—
of figs unsweet yet, yet beryl-bright
enough for wonder.

Not jackdaw, but not different, I—how I destroy myself
on even the least of the sweetest things—
the salt of her burned not long on my tongue,
but like stars.

I never meant to break—but love,
the hymn and bells of her.

Even now, there are nights I climb the narrow stairway
to an apartment at Hradčany Square, where a door opens
to a room and the shadowed fig of her mouth—
cleaved sweet open, and in me ringing.

Vicki Feaver

1974

The year Anne Sexton
sat in her red Cougar
with a glass of vodka
behind the closed doors
of her garage and drifted off
to its purring lullaby
in her mother's fur coat.

The year I read Emily Dickinson:
'This is the Hour of Lead –
Remembered, if outlived,
As Freezing persons, recollect the Snow –
First – Chill – then Stupor – then, the letting go –'

'What do you do?'
a man asked me at a party.
'What do you do in the afternoons?'

I was thirty-one:
the same age as Plath
when she turned on the gas.

'I'm a poet!' I lied
jolting myself to life:
a woman buried under ice
with words burning inside.

The Larder

Yesterday it was the blaze
of a broom bush; the day before

the peppermint whiff
of a beeswax lip-balm.

Each day, I fill the shelves
with things to remember.

Today, it's the powdery bloom
on the skin of a blueberry,

turning it, cold from the fridge,
between my thumb and finger;

noticing the petal-shaped crater
where the flower withered

and the small hole
where it was pulled

from the stalk; crushing
its tangy pulp on my tongue.

David Morley

After the Burial of the Gypsy Matriarch

marime vôrdòn

The Roma are torching her proud vardo in mirnomos.
The yag leaps into the bóro and billows in mirnomos.
Páto, tsáliya, pátura: her possessions flare in mirnomos.
Her raklo shuffles her bánka, palms them out in mirnomos.
The yag leaps into the bóro and billows in mirnomos.

Her lurcher is nashaval from the kámpo in mirnomos.
Her raklo shuffles her bánka, palms them out in mirnomos.
The zhukûl peers and peers from the wûsh in mirnomos.
Her lurcher is nashaval from the kámpo in mirnomos.
Pàrrâ towers to its kríza, collapses in mirnomos.

The zhukûl peers and peers from the wûsh in mirnomos.
The Roma rake and rake the skrúma in mirnomos.
Pàrrâ towers to its kríza, collapses in mirnomos.
Their vardos circle the field. They vanish in mirnomos.
The Roma rake and rake the skrúma in mirnomos.

What the Roma do not say to each other is buried in mirnomos.
Their vardos circle the field. They vanish in mirnomos.
Páto, tsáliya, pátura: everything burns in mirnomos.
What the Roma do not say to each other is buried in mirnomos.
The Roma are torching her vardo. Everything must burn.

After death, the home and belongings of a Roma Gypsy are considered mahrime, 'unclean', and are burnt. **Romani: English: marime vôrdòn:** contaminated wagon; **vardo:** Gypsy caravan; **mirnomos:** silence; **yag:** fire; **bóro:** oak; **páto:** bed; **tsáliya:** clothing; **pátura:** bedclothes; **raklo:** son; **bánka:** banknotes; **nashaval:** chased away; **kámpo:** camp; **zhukûl:** hound; **wûsh:** woodland; **pàrrâ:** flames; **kríza:** crisis; **skrúma:** ashes.

FURY

I love talking.
Tyson Fury, British Romany professional boxer

The fight's over. My corner-man and cut-man
are mist and water, mist and slaughter.
I scream at the crowd and swagger to the exit.
I bow my face in a locker-room mirror,
and to the mirror behind my eyes.
Infinity. A million beaten faces
stare out, blazing back at me,
brains black-puddinged from pummelling.
My fists are beating the locker door.
I am fighting-royalty. I have Gypsy
kings on both sides of the family.
My three brothers are the same as me.
With us, everyone is a tough guy.
They don't talk like you and me
are talking. But we all cry instantly.
Look at me: 6 feet 9. If someone
said this to me in my family,
I would just cry. All of us would.
But nothing's talked about in our family.
We just push each other aside,
or give each other a punch.
We don't bow to any man.
The red mist rises, an invisible
cloak around my ringside robe.
We won't bow to you.
I bow to the red mist, naked as fury.
It's not about the money fights.
It's the love of one-on-one combat,
the ring entrances, the talking.
I'm the Master of It all.
When I go in there, I'm trying
to put my fist through the back

of his head. To break his ribs,
make them sob out the other side.
Final bell. I bow to the mist, being gone.
I feel a chill burning my skin.
When the red mist rises, I see
their faces, as many as my mind's eye
can remember. I'd give my right arm
for any man who stays on his toes.
I'm in control when out of control.
The best style is no style.
You take a little something from everything,
use what works, chuck the rest out the ring.
My game's to get your man on the ground –
sprawl-and-brawl, grind-and-pound.
Gum-shield and teeth, they're one to me.
Once down, don't get up from your knees.
This is not your celeb boxing.
It's felling the other chancer in the ring
short of butchering the bastard
before he gets his breath back,
before he begs for no more.
One clean blow and the mist
will part for him. My opponent begs
for mercy. What's that, pal?
I'm Fury. Who's this Mercy?
The breath goes up from the beaten
ghost of a man. Submission.
I'll tell you who Fury is.
Eye to eyeball at the mirror;
breath on the screen while I scream
at replays on my iPad.
Pal,
one minute I'm inside the sun
and the next I'm in my car, gunning it
into a wall at a hundred miles an hour.
I don't trust you as far as I could
throw you. I don't trust myself.

I bought a brand-new Ferrari
in the summer of 2016.
I was bombing up the motorway
got the beast up to 190mph
heading smack towards a bridge.
I heard a voice crying,
your kids, your family,
your sons and daughter
growing up without their dad.
Before I turned into the bridge
I skidded back on the hard shoulder.
I have been so dark everything was pitch-black.
The fight's over. My corner-man and cut-man
are mist and water, mist and slaughter.
There is a name for what I am. I scream it
at the crowd and stagger to the exit.

Pascale Petit

Green Bee-eater

More precious than all
the gems of Jaipur –

the green bee-eater.

If you see one singing
tree-tree-tree

with his space-black bill
and rufous cap,

his robes
all shades of emerald

like treetops glimpsed
from a plane,

his blue cheeks,
black eye-mask

and the delicate tail streamer
like a plume of smoke –

you might dream
of the forests

that once clothed
our flying planet.

And perhaps his singing
is a spell

to call our forests back –

tree
    by *tree*
         by *tree.*

Tiger Gran

My grandmother of the flying electric blanket,
who speaks Hindi in her sleep,
who has gharials in her black eyes
behind steamed-up glasses, a long nose
like a mountain between two countries – one hot, one cold.
Who mothered me when I was newborn,
and saved me from going to the bad.

My grandmother who returned me to my mother twice,
which meant orphanage, which meant other people's homes.
My grandmother who took me back
for seven years from age seven, who saved my life,
praise to the mothering of my tigress!
My grandmother who works at the chippie, who takes in
neighbours' washing, who cleans big houses,

who makes me work in the garden for my keep,
for whom I would weed the world,
for whom I would pump the Severn to save her black hybrids,
for she is a hybrid rose who has been saved.
My grandmother who keeps a jungle folded in her greenhouse,
who lets me join her in its heat-heart.
My grandmother whom I catch peeing among the plant pots,

who explains she has only one kidney
and can't always make it to our toilet.
My grandmother whose hair fell out
when they removed her kidney without anaesthetic
while she was pregnant with my uncle.
My grandmother who shouts *Avert your eyes!* when she undresses,
so I won't see the permanent tan under her clothes.

My grandmother with the curse of second sight
but the blessing of second birth to her father's wife
so her real mother, the maid, would not be stoned.
My grandmother who was left alone in a jungle tent
by her white step-mother, for the tiger to eat,
who, when we are riding the winged blanket,
tells me how she watched the vision enter

and reached out to touch its dazzle, who was spared
because she was not afraid, who held
the wonder's gaze and saw its icicle teeth drip
on the red tongue at the gate of paradise
but did not go down that carpet into the tunnel.
My tawny grandma with as many wrinkles as tributaries
in the Ganges, her face the map of India when it's summer,

the map of Wales in winter. And sometimes her wrinkles
are stripes that scare me if I look at her
when she is flying the tails of her stories.
She who was left to run wild by her doting father
when she wasn't slaving for his white family,
who I am allowed to cuddle so I can sleep.
My grandmother the tiger-girl. The Untouchable.

Shortlisted Poems
The Felix Dennis Prize
for Best First Collection

Ella Frears

Fucking in Cornwall

The rain is thick and there's half a rainbow
over the damp beach; just put your hand up my top.

I've walked around that local museum a hundred times
and I've decided that the tiny, stuffed dog,
labelled *the smallest dog in the world*, is a fake.

Kiss me in a pasty shop with all the ovens on.

I've held a warm, new egg on a farm and thought about fucking.
I've held a tiny green crab in the palm of my hand.

I've pulled my sleeve over my fingers and picked a nettle
and held it to a boy's throat like a sword.

Unlace my shoes in that alley and lift me gently onto the bins.

The bright morning sun is coming and coming
and the holiday children have their yellow buckets ready.

Do you remember what it felt like to dig a hole all day
with a plastic spade just to watch it fill with sea?

I want it like that – like water feeling its way over
an edge. Like two bright-red anemones in a rock pool,
tentacles waving ecstatically.

Like the gorse has caught fire across the moors and you
are the ghost of a fisherman who always hated land.

Sestina for Caroline Bergvall

I stood in front of an installation by Caroline Bergvall.
I was struck, not only by the text but by her voice
which had the clarity of running water but also an edge
of music – romance, like someone throwing a rose over their
shoulder, to no one in particular & without looking back.
Heading home, I resisted that bittersweet bus sleep.

Once nestled between three free hours though, I did sleep
& dreamed my house was grand & Caroline Bergvall
came for tea. Having never seen her, it was just the back
of her head ... the back of *a* head. But I knew her voice.
She pointed to a balcony with no balustrade. *There.*
In dreams I'm always heading towards an edge –

a cliff, a smashed plate, a kerb – though this edge
could be, and probably is, just the end of sleep.
The more I scrubbed the teacups, the more grime there
was inside. I was worried that Caroline Bergvall
was bored but when I apologised for the delay, her voice
came out of my mouth. And then ... I was back

on the bus, the warmth of the engine – the backs
of many heads ahead of me. Driving towards an edge.
I felt it. I wondered which head contained her voice.
Why a bus? I asked no one. *Is it a metaphor for sleep?*
Driven by the subconscious until we reach our stop. Bergvall
was silent, or maybe she wasn't there.

Then, looking at the rows of heads – an epiphany – *they're*
all Caroline Bergvall! Caroline Bergvall with the pink back-
pack, Caroline Bergvall with the centre parting, Bergvall
with the tonsure & cane, little Bergvall on the edge
of her seat naming things, Bergvall asleep
surrounded by shopping bags, Bergvall hearing voices.

The bus hurtled on, listing the stops in Bergvall's voice
& I feared the destination less – we were all headed there
together. If language can be disrupted by sleep,
then what is a word but the vehicle we drive back
& forth – letters, texts, emails we leave behind, the edge
of who we are; the back of a head – never the full Bergvall.

Asleep, I throw my voice over my shoulder. *Bless us!*
Every Bergvall, here, there & on the bus. & bless these inadequate
words, thrown back, as we step off the edge.

Will Harris

My Name Is Dai

I heard him say his name was die, and seconds later that it was short for David, spelt *D-A-I*. We had just sat down when he walked up to me and Susie. He said he recognised her from the National Portrait Gallery. The one with the large forehead above the door. People miss it.

The sad
smile. Beer sloshed against the edges of his glass like a fish trying to escape its bowl, but in this case the fish was dead and only looked to be alive because of Dai's swaying. There are people who relieve themselves of information like a dog pissing against a streetlamp to mark out territory, urination no longer in the service of the body, providing no relief. Likewise, conversation. Dai was a type of Ancient Mariner.

It was in his bones. He'd been working on a site with Polish builders and it was one of their birthdays. He mimed plunking bottles on the
table.
Vodka. Whole bottles? *I'm Welsh*, he said. *I was born on a mountain. Between two sheepdogs.* He started talking about the village he grew up in, how happy he was among the meadows and milking cows, how unhappy he was at school. *You might've heard of one boy from school. A right goody. Spoke like Audrey Hepburn or Shakespeare. We all bullied him, but my mam would say why don't you be like Michael, why don't you be like Michael. Michael bloody Sheen. Michael's shirts were always clean and ironed. Anthony Hopkins, he was a local too. A tiny village,*

and who came out of it? Those two and me. You know, I probably know more words than anyone in this pub. Look at them. You think any of these cunts can spell verbiage? He spat out each letter – *V-E-R-B-I-A-G-E* – and in the act of spelling became self-conscious. He turned to Susie. *What do you do?* She was a writer so he told her more words. I said I taught a little and wrote. *Teach me*, he said. *Go on.* But I couldn't think of
anything wise or useful to tell Dai. On the verge of tipping over, he held a hand out towards us. *Tenderness*, he said, *try a little tenderness,*

and then repeating it, half singing it, he said it in a voice both louder and more tender. *That's my advice. You know who that is? Otis Redding.*

Try a little tenderness, mmm nuh uh uh. That was when Susie saw the haze descend. Like an explosion in a quarry the inward collapse rippled out across his face, throwing clouds of dust into the sky. *I'm sorry. A man shouldn't cry. I haven't cried since I was a boy. I haven't ...* He stopped. *A man should be a brick, a boulder.* He made his hand into a fist like he was playing rock-paper-scissors in the schoolyard. *My ex-wife died last month. The funeral was yesterday. We were together twenty years but her family, her bloody family, wouldn't let me near it. God,* he said, *I loved that woman.* He couldn't say her name. He was swaying. I got the impression that he saw

his life as a sea voyage during which he'd done many strange, inexplicable
and stupid things, of which shooting an albatross was one. But perhaps he knew it was better to have shot that albatross through the heart and be able to talk about it than to bear it having entered his life and gone. It was then I saw the TV and pointed. *Look! Michael Sheen.* It was true. There he was on *The One Show* in a freshly ironed shirt, smiling at Matt Baker. Dai turned around. *I'm sorry. I don't know what came over me. I need some air.* He stared at us. *You're writers,* he said. *You should write about this.* And though it may have been unfair, I thought about how many people he'd said this to before.

Yellow

*The 'marvellous Chinese conjurer' Chung Ling Soo, born William
Ellsworth Robinson, died on 24 March 1918 attempting to catch
a bullet on stage. He had modelled his appearance and act on the
contemporary Chinese magician Ching Ling Foo, born Zhu Liankui
(朱連魁), who died in 1922.*

Think of Chung Ling Soo who,
a century ago, his smooth
face greased and pigtail
bobbing, brought the wonders
of the East to the London
Hippodrome. A blend
of grace and speed, his face
impassive as a clay
soldier's, he was an early
master of the linking rings
and wove a braid so fine
they say he made of it
a gift to the Empress
Dowager.

Now think of
Ching Ling Foo, a conjurer
from Peking who one day
browsing through the news
caught sight of Soo's
impassive face (his own
but strange) and went to
London – midwinter, mid-
Depression, fog so thick
the rooftops looked like they
were under sea – to call
his double out. Drunk suitors
followed day and night,

pulling at his hair. He did
two shows. No one came.
He grew impatient, wrote in
bluntly to *The Times*, then
turned a row of empty
seats into a flock of geese
and disappeared.

          Now think of
Soo and Foo at the same time
but separately: a blue sky
as reflected in a clear blue lake,
water above and water
below. There's Soo doubled-
over on stage, gun smoke
clearing, real blood running
down his long silk shirt,
shouting *Lower the curtain!*
A nasal brogue (his own
but strange) rings through
the theatre, fades.

          Somewhere
in a corner of the Yellow
River Valley, Foo is sleeping
underneath a pinkish plum tree,
dreaming he's suspended
by his ankles in a sealed
water tank, pigtail floating
up across his eyes. He tries
to pull the loose knot free
but only pulls it tighter.
Bound and gagged he feels
the muscles slacken
from the back of his neck
down to his anus, his

calves, his anonymous
toes, around which billows
the yellow squit of his
final movement.

Rachel Long

The Omen

Dad said that when Mum first walked into class
she wore a question mark on her head.
A question mark? We laugh.

Yeah, it was sort of all brushed up on top of her head,
a plait thing sticking up, and she would pin one end down
like a question mark – on top of her head.

Ignore that man! Mum shouts from the kitchen.

Red Hoover

He was ridiculously good-looking. He was even Nigerian
– though Mum flits between this being a good thing in people
and the worst. I pulled his photo up on the internet, showed her.
She decided, on the spot, his Nigerianness was a good thing.
It was easy to pull his photo up on the internet
because he was an actor. I'd met him in a theatre.
He'd just been awarded a £3000 cheque
for being a Nigerian actor. It was a very hot summer.
I wore a black playsuit belonging to my younger sister
but carried a blazer – for a look that said: serious play.
He offered to buy me a drink. Of course
I said I'd prefer to buy my own, and when he insisted
I said OK like it was quite inconvenient for me to agree.
When our drinks were on the bar and glistening
in the velvet heat, he handed the barman his cheque.
Ha ha ha, said the barman. Ha ha ha, I said.
So, the ridiculously good-looking Nigerian had jokes.

On my lunchbreak, I found a clean bench to call him from.
We were awkward. I wanted him to ask me out.
Why wasn't he asking me out? Mum began asking after him,
where's that good-looking Nigerian? Don't tell me
you've ruined it already.

The second time, I spread out on my bed,
swung my legs up the wall – cold and good for my nerves.
It was a short call because someone was knocking at his door.
OK I said like it was of no inconvenience whatsoever.
I slid my legs back down the wall.

A week later, I was standing in his living room
wearing my coat, or it was over my arm, my shoes still on.
Either, we were just about to go out, or I'd just arrived
and he hadn't yet said, *Here, let me take your coat*
or, *Please, take off your shoes.*

He was running all over the house.
Upstairs then down, zooming around.
He was running a bath, then letting the water out
only to fill it back up. He ducked into a cupboard
and yanked a hoover. A red hoover.
He began hoovering everywhere,
he even hoovered the ceiling.
He just walked up the wall
and as he did, looked over his shoulder,
at me on the floor and said,
this won't take long, I just have to —

When I told Mum, she shook her head, laughed –
half lemon, half sugar. He's crazy, she shrugged,
God's showing you it won't work out because
he's all over the place. Shame. That good-looking man …
Nigerians, she sighed, always into something.

I'd still look him up on the Internet sometimes.
Just to keep up to date with his plays, the BBC dramas.
Then I stopped. For years I didn't think of him.
OK, perhaps, but in a loose and smirking way;
playful, no serious pining. What was there to pine really?
Then, in bed one night, watching an OK adaptation
on my laptop, the ridiculously good-looking Nigerian
walks across the screen. His name escapes my mouth;
half sigh, half whistle. I say it like damn. I say it like,
man, where have you been? He has a few lines
then he's stabbed on a street I recognise
having danced down a long time ago.
Long before I met him at that theatre,
with his cheque folded into his pocket.
I remember our two awkward phone calls
and him hoovering his ceiling
and I laugh into my pillow
as he bleeds out.

Nina Mingya Powles

Conversational Chinese

[Please fill in the blanks by choosing the correct word from the list below.]

She was born in _____ in _____. She escaped to the Malaysian peninsula when she was _____ years old. Her father _____ _____. From a young age she helped her mother farm the land. She began learning a little English _____ _____. In _____ she married a handsome marine biology student. She had three children, two daughters and one son, all of whom attended the local Christian Chinese school. In the evenings she sat under the _____ tree in her backyard, rinsing and peeling _____ into a _____ bowl, watching her youngest son chase her eldest daughter around the grass with a cicada tied to the end of a piece of string. Some years later, when the _____ started up in the streets, she looked at the sea and longed to send her children across it, far away, where they would be _____, where she would one day visit them.

Shenzhen / Guangzhou / Xiamen / 1928 / 1929 / 1931
five / six / nine / eight
died shortly after / did not join them / fell ill on board
in high school / from a stranger / by teaching herself
1953 / 1954 / 1956 / mango / breadfruit / yellow flame
coconut / fresh ginger / turmeric root / daikon / wintermelon
turquoise / aquamarine / seafoam
sirens / shouting / loudspeakers / fires
in her prayers / happy / safe

[Please answer the following questions in full sentences.]

你的外婆在哪里出生？
Mum says it isn't really clear where she was born, but most likely somewhere near Shenzhen.

你的外婆什么时候来到马来西亚？
We think she came by boat along with her mother and father, but we think her father may have died on the journey, or somehow didn't make it.

你的外婆在哪里入土为安？
They scattered her ashes over the sea off the coast of Kota Kinabalu, within sight of the blue mountain made of clouds.

Sonnet with particles of gold

Today scientists discovered the origins of gold:
the sound of egg noodles crisping up in the wok,
the garden carpeted in kōwhai petals,
the way my phone corrects raumati (*summer*) to *rainstorm*.
The day after my grandmother died was white-gold in colour.
A star explodes and wings are found among the debris
along with pieces of a character I never memorised –
our only name for her, 婆, a woman 女 beneath a wave 波.
"Drift," she mouths softly in English, "what is *drift*?"
My mother translates into her language, not one of mine.
I try to make myself remember by writing 婆 over and over
on squares of paper covering the walls so I am surrounded
by the women and the water radicals they hold close.
The tips of waves touch me in my sleep.

Martha Sprackland

Pimientos de Padrón

Os pementos de Padrón
uns pican e outros non

A plateful of dark green bullets
slick in their lake of grassy blood
and charred from the fire,

still hissing and settling, smoking,
the skin lifting and curling
studded with salt-flakes.

They were our cheap roulette – *some hot,*
others not (the capsicum is brewed
by the sudden sun at summer's edge).

We were all of us bad at decisions,
lovesick, shamed or fleeing
or brisant and in shock. The city emptied

as the madrileños boarded up
the bodegas and rippled out
towards the cooler coasts

leaving us to our own boiling ghosts,
reckless enough to hold
the dare to our mouths, fire

or sweetness spreading across the tongue
and then head to the airport
for the first flight anywhere but home.

Tooth

Like a round grey stone lodged
in the fork of a tree
the tooth sits intractably
at the far back of the mouth
between the ear and the jaw.

The mouth can't close fully,
like a freezer door;
can't crank itself open
more than a few gear-teeth's width,
enough for water through a straw.

At night it wakes up
like an eyeball, lolls sourly on the tongue
rolls against the drum
tampers with the hinge
and rubs it raw.

Nothing to do, between the shift-
change of the painkillers
but listen to my bedmate
breathing asleep and the foghorns
in the hot harbour.

All the world's cameras
are on this clamorous point:
this knot, this bole, this clot,
this breaking news, this fire,
this prisoner of war,

a sealed world seething
like a black egg
incorruptible by amoxicillin
and saline wash.
I want it out.

I go down to the dockside,
oily between the cruise ships
and Maersk containers,
to gargle palmfuls of the sea
against the hard bezoar

and its faulty magic.
I idle towards
the half-bottle of whiskey,
the red-handled relief
in the kitchen drawer,

but Ed shifts and turns against me,
skin like cotton, outside the pain,
and says through sleep –
his clean sound mouth –
Honey, are you still sore?

I can't answer
round the cobblestone,
the ship, the choke, the pliers,
the acorn cracked
and pushing through the floor.

Shortlisted Poems
The Forward Prize for Best Single Poem

Fiona Benson

Mama Cockroach, I Love You

Blattodea

Because you cosy with the aunties in your
reeking slums, and are intimate and sweet.

Because you begrudge no one a meal, but ooze
a faecal trail to lead your commune to its source,

like a dirty bee. Because you are joyfully promiscuous.
Because you pouch your young and hide them

in the sweaty creases of the house
near suppurating food so they'll hatch to a feast;

or, keep your eggs with you in a special purse
shaped like a kidney bean, and clutch it fast;

or reinsert them into your abdomen
and womb them there; or carry them as yolks

and give live birth, then feed your pale brood
secretions from your anus, or your armpit glands,

like milk; or, deep in the flesh of a rotten log
pass them a bolus of pre-digested food, mouth to mouth.

Because you suffer your young to swarm upon
your back, and do not flinch or buck them off,

but carry them like a human playing horsey
with her children, down on hands and knees,

decrying the swag of her own loose flesh.
Because you twirl your antennae gracefully

to test your crawl space. Because strokingly
you caress your offspring's backs, and gentle them

with pretty pheromones and chirps. Because
you purr when your young stroke your face.

Because you would leave your body for your offspring
to dine upon – all the liquors and gravy

of the obscene world, your work in the crannies
delivered to the living. Because you are,

despite all rumours, mortal. And what if
you are crushed before your eggs can be delivered?

What if your sisters drive you, hissing, out?
What if your kitchen is fumigated?!

What if the mongoose the lizard the snake –
a muscular tongue prying at the warm and greasy interstices

of your stubborn occupancy – takes you in its mouth?
Someone must care for the dirt.

Malika Booker

The Little Miracles

After 'A Winter Night' by Tomas Tranströmer
(translated by Robin Robertson)

Since I found mother collapsed on the kitchen
floor, we siblings have become blindfolded mules

harnessed to carts filled with strain, lumbering
through a relentless storm, wanting to make

our mother walk on her own again, wanting to rest
our palms on her left leg and arm like Jesus, but

constellations do not gather like leaves in a teacup,
so what miracle, of what blood, of what feeble wishes

do we pray, happy no nails hammer plywood, building
a coffin, to house her dead weight, happy her journey

crawls as we her children hold on like drought holds out
for rain, learning what it is like to begin again, start

with the, the, the dog, the cat, the date, the year, the
stroke, the brain, the fenced in walls, she struggles

to dismantle brick on brick. *She cannot break this,*
we reason, watching her left hand in her lap, a useless

echo. We chew bitter bush, swallow our howling storm,
reluctantly splintering under the strain of our mother's

ailing bed-rest. We smile at each of her feats: right hand
brushing her teeth in late evening, head able to lift

without the aid of a neck-brace, her offspring's names
Malika, Phillip and Kwesi are chants repeated over

and over as if staking us children as her life's work,
her blessings, showing how much we are loved. The days

she sings *walk with me oh my Lord,* over and over, *walk
with me oh my Lord, through the darkest night...* and I sing

with her, my tones flat to her soprano, *just as you changed
the wind and walked upon the sea, conquer, my living Lord,*

the storm that threatens me, and we sing and sing until
she says, *Maliks, please stop the cat-wailing before*

*you voice mek rain fall, and look how the weather nice
outside eh!* Then we laugh and laugh until almost giddy,

our mood light momentarily in this sterile room, where
each spoonful of pureed food slipped into her mouth

like a tender offering takes us a step away from feeding
tubes, and we are so thankful for each minuscule miracle.

Regi Claire

(Un)certainties

My sister once gave me
A. an ultramarine silk scarf
B. a star-shaped candlestick of clear glass
C. a guardian angel made from clay and driftwood

My sister loved
A. her family
B. her partner
C. kayaks

My sister's partner loved
A. her
B. his family
C. kayaks

My sister and her partner loved
A. adventure
B. sports
C. water
D. the sea

My sister and her partner
A. had been on sea kayaking trips before
B. were familiar with that coastline
C. were offered a guided tour
D. trusted their abilities and experience

My sister sent her children
A. a WhatsApp message saying how excited she was about that
    day's 10 km kayaking trip
B. a picture of the mirror-smooth sea
C. a selfie in a swim vest
D. emojis of dolphins

My sister's postcard to our parents
A. was sent before the kayaking trip
B. was sent by hotel staff after the kayaking trip
C. arrived ten days after the kayaking trip, before her funeral

My sister died
A. on Friday 13th
B. on Saturday 14th

My sister's partner did not die
A. on Friday 13th
B. on Saturday 14th

My sister died at sea, alone
A. soon after sunset in a storm
B. in the dark in a storm
C. at dawn, after a storm
D. in sunlight, on the morning after a storm

My sister's partner clung to his kayak at sea, alone
A. from sunset to false dawn throughout a storm
B. from sunset to sunrise throughout a storm and the calm
   hours beyond
C. from sunset to sunlit morning throughout a storm and the
   calm hours beyond

My sister died because
A. she and her partner spent time on a series of beaches along
   the coast, picnicking, shell-gathering, sunbathing, resting
B. she and her partner spent time exploring the disused
   submarine tunnel under the cliffs
C. she was afraid of the dark inside the tunnel and so she sang,
   seated in her kayak as her partner listened, sang her heart out
   for the soaring echo of it, and the echo could not bear to lose
   her and her voice

My sister died because
A. the mirror smoothness of the water began to break,
   and broken mirrors bring bad luck
B. the waves were too small to seem alarming
C. the waves grew in strength only slowly

My sister died because
A. the land weather forecast was wrong
B. the sea weather forecast was wrong

My sister died because
A. she was first to round the headland, where the wind bore
   down on her from the mountains and whipped up the waves
B. her partner, some distance behind, saw her being driven off-
   course and decided to follow
C. the wind kept their kayaks apart, barely within shouting
   range, while the sun went down
D. her partner capsized and, holding on with his chin and both
   hands, could only watch as the sky darkened to storm-black
   and she sat upright in her kayak, cresting the waves out into
   the open sea

My sister and her partner
A. knew their GPS
B. knew they were a kilometre at most from the headland
C. could see the village with their hotel further down the coast

My sister and her partner managed to use their mobiles to contact
A. the kayak rental owner
B. the local police
C. the police in the neighbouring country
D. the coast guard

The last thing my sister and her partner told each other was

A. at least we've seen the sunset from out at sea, not just from the beach
B. I love you
C. let's not panic
D. help is coming

Half a year earlier, my sister and her partner had visited an Indonesian sanctuary for retired elephants, which they helped wash in the nearby stream, getting soaked to the skin.

Half a lifetime earlier, she and her husband had given their babies a bath every night, getting soaked to the skin.

A lifetime earlier, she and I had played in the stream next to our house, catching tadpoles and damming the water with pebbles, twigs and mud, getting soaked to the skin.

My sister died

A. because she capsized
B. because she lost her kayak
C. because she lost hope
D. from the intake of too much sea water
E. from exhaustion
F. in panic
G. in peace

My sister died because

A. the kayak rental owner did not have a motorboat for emergencies
B. the kayak rental owner told her and her partner to phone the local police
C. it was the weekend and the police were short-staffed
D. there was no coast guard

E. there were no helicopters
F. the passengers on the regular ferry services did not notice the torchlight from her partner's mobile as he moved it in circles above his head until the battery was flat
G. the coast guard of the neighbouring country arrived too late

My sister was found
A. 5 hours after the storm began
B. 10 hours after the storm began
C. 16 hours after the storm began

My sister was found
A. near the coast
B. 15 km away
C. 25 km away, close to the beaches of a small island advertised for family holidays

My sister's partner was rescued after clinging to his kayak
A. for 5 hours
B. for 10 hours
C. for 15 hours

My sister and her partner were found
A. near each other
B. in separate locations

My sister's partner was taken
A. to his hotel
B. to a local hospital
C. to a hospital on an island in the neighbouring country

My sister's partner
A. was only slightly injured
B. had nerve damage to one hand
C. would make a complete physical recovery
D. would never fully recover

My sister's partner had
A. no phone numbers for her family
B. no phone numbers for his children
C. to wait for his mobile to dry out in a bag of uncooked rice before he could get any phone numbers
D. to use someone else's mobile
E. to use a pay phone

My sister's partner was visited in hospital
A. by his children
B. by his Consul General
C. by an ambulance chaser

After my sister and her partner were found, the kayak rental owner contacted the helpline of the Department of Foreign Affairs of their home country
A. to report the accident
B. to inform them of the death and injury
C. to request compensation for the lost kayak

My parents were notified
A. later than the Department of Foreign Affairs
B. later than local and international news media

Several months after my sister's funeral her partner
A. returned to the country where the accident had happened, to complete the photography commission that had originally taken him there
B. visited the kayak rental owner
C. undertook another kayaking trip by himself along the same coast
D. started a new relationship

My sister's partner died
A. 6 months after the storm
B. 12 months after the storm
C. 15 months to the day after the storm

My sister's partner died
A. on Saturday 12th
B. on Sunday 13th

My sister's partner died
A. of a massive heart attack
B. of a broken heart
C. of heart strain caused by the accident
D. of congenital heart disease

My sister and her partner are
A. buried in the same cemetery
B. buried near each other in the same cemetery
C. not buried in the same cemetery

My sister's cat
A. never slept on her bed
B. stayed on my sister's bed in the empty house for several
    months after her death, fed by neighbours
C. did not die the following summer

At my sister's funeral I met a distraught young man she had
supported with therapy sessions.
'But where did your sister die?' he asked. 'Where? What is the
name of the town? The place?'
When I tried to explain, he did not understand.
Could not.

Valzhyna Mort

Nocturne for a Moving Train

The trees I've glimpsed from the window
of a night train were
the saddest trees.

They seemed about to speak,
then –
      vanished like soldiers.

The hostesses handed out starched linens for sleep.
Passengers bent over small icons
of sandwiches.

In a tall glass, a spoon mixed sugar into coffee
banging its silver face against the facets.

The window reflected back a figure
struggling with white sheets.

The posts with names of towns promised
a possibility of words
for what flew by.

In lit-up windows people seemed to move
as if performing surgery on tables.

Chestnut parks sighed the sighs of creatures
capable of speech.

Radiation, an etymology of soil

directed into the future, prepared
a thesis on the new origins of old roots,

on secret, disfiguring missions of misspellings,
on the shocking betrayal of apples,
on the uncompromised loyalty of cesium.

My childish voice, my hands, my feet – all my things that live
on the edges of me –
shhh now, the chestnut parks are about to speak.

But now they've vanished.

I was extracted from my apartment block,
chained to the earth with iron playgrounds,
where iron swings rose like oil wells,

I was extracted before I could dig a language
out of air
with my childish feet.

I was extracted by beaks – storks, cranes.

See, the conductor punching out eyes
of sleeping passengers.
What is it about my face
that turns it into a document,
into a ticket stretched out by a neck?

Why does unfolding this starched bedding
feel like
                    skinning someone invisible?
Why can't the spoons, head-down in glasses, stop screaming?

Shhh…

The chestnuts are about to speak.

Sarah Tsiang

Dick pics

Two dicks, sitting in
my daughter's inbox.
Like men without hats,
waiting for any door
to open.

*

Sighting a stranger's penis
used to be rare. Remember raincoats?
Like a flash of lightning,
like a scratch and win ticket –
sometimes glittering knock-off watches,
sometimes a sole flapping penis
shivering in the electric air.

*

An overcooked hotdog?
An aborted fetus?
A close-up of a thumb?
Rolled baloney on a lonely deli plate?

*

We have whole monologues
for vaginas. But I can only imagine
a penis as silent,
which isn't the same
as listening.

*

The lighting is never
good. Harsh, taken in haste,
no one ever drapes
a dick in folds of linen,

the head never looks
back, one pearl earring
shining in stilled patience.

*

On every tunnel,
school yard, crumbling brick wall,
a graffitied cock, standing on balls
pointing to the night sky,
like a fallen constellation.

*

Women were for portraits, nudes
lounging, stuffed into frames,
luminous and arch. They were heads
and breasts, and feet, and buttocks
(though never speech). You must pay
and cross a velvet rope to see them.

The penis stood alone, in filthy
bars, and bathrooms, in wooded
parks, in the shadowed alleys
whistling a moon-white tune.

*

Now every penis is everywhere.
Like posters for a one-act play,
plastered on every telephone pole,
bench, building, on every mailbox,
on your kitchen chair,

so that you have to push through piles of them,
great snowdrifts of penises,
just to reach across the room
and tuck a stray hair
back into your daughter's braid.

Highly Commended Poems

Juana Adcock

The Guitar's Lament

I recently reached the conclusion that I am a guitar.
There were numerous clues that suggested the above, but
        until now
I had lived blind to them.

Firstly there are of course my handsome curves
the resonant hollow in my chest
my stiff arms
the tension of strings that keep me tied
to who knows what hair-raising notes of the past.

To that we must add my ability to align my body
against that of a musician
my fondness for the numbers 5 and 12
my being able to sound only when strummed
my inevitable position as an object
my connection to balconies and bad poets
my repeatability in simple chords
my dusty fretboard
my fixed form
my frustration at not being a hat
or a bird
or a tree
or a violin at least.

Every day I rise early for work
hang from a wall
or a shoulder
or sit on a knee
and repeat the phrases of the dead
phrases that are not mine
lever of the histrionic
ancient shell.

One thought and only one
brings me solace: that endings are mere artifice.
Nothing starts or ends. Not even I
started at my navel or end at my skin

Romalyn Ante

Kayumanggi

Remember the myth – the night you lifted your arm
to the light, adoring the *kayumanggi*-gleam of your skin –

how God moulded people from clay. He was hasty once,
not firing the first clump of clay-men long enough,

then careless for burning the next batch. Turn your back
on the brash-blinking tarmac, on the next-door lad

on a narra ladder who festoons festive lights, and yells
with a lancet-sharp snigger, *Ang itim! You're ugly!*

If a shadow of a teak tree spills and pins you at your feet,
remember darkness is neither the absence of light

nor the abundance of shades. Might as well let bygones
be bygones – the bucket that bobbed in a brimming tub

and you, the ugly duckling who scrubbed and scrubbed.
Go ahead – trail that next-door boy and mock his body

glazed in sewage sludge after a ladder fall. Soon,
a whistle pulls you to a bench. The breeze persuades

a hanging lantern. Memorise your mother's story
of God's endurance, and learn that on his third try

he gaped at the last batch of clay people
and was satisfied.

Dean Atta

The Making

after Shailja Patel

Make it out of those scraps of attention
your father scattered across your timeline.
The two times he came to see you on stage.
The one time he visited you at university.
Gather them and add to the scrapbook
of love, advice and guidance from uncles.
How Uncle D told you a relationship relies
on compromise. How Uncle T showed you
that even when falling apart you can still make
small but significant repairs for others.

Make your mother the spine to this book.
Make it sing kind words. Make it to find out
what words can fix and what they cannot.
Make it for your mother's approval. Make it
selfishly sometimes. Make it in secret, in public,
in meditation and prayer. Make it a prayer.
Pray to the earth, the universe, the light inside
yourself. Make it a mantra. Make it to forgive,
yourself. Make it to fix what's been broken.
When you break, make no apologies.

Sue Hyon Bae

After the Threesome, They Both Take You Home

even though it's so very late
and they have to report to jobs
in a few hours, they both get in the car,
one driving, one shotgun, you in the back
like a child needing a drive to settle into sleep,
even though one could drive and the other
sleep, because they can't
without each other, they'd rather drive you
across the city than be apart for even a half hour,
the office buildings lit pointlessly beautiful
for nobody except you to admire the reflections
in the water, the lovers too busy talking
about that colleague they don't like,
tomorrow's dinner plans, how once
they bought peaches on a road trip and ate and ate
until they could taste it in each other's pores,
they get out of the car together to kiss you goodnight,
you who have perfected the ghost goodbye,
exiting gatherings noiselessly, leaving only
a dahlia-scented perfume, your ribcage
compressing to slide untouched through doors ajar,
yesterday you were a flash of white in a pigeon's blinking eye,
in the day a few hours old you stand solid and full
of other people's love for each other
spilling over, warm leftovers.

Tessa Berring

An Intention to Be Present

I bought a bathmat
on Sunday morning

the equivalent

of not worshipping God
at exactly the same time

I needed to soap myself

to peel things off
and not slip over

I love the way Veronica
puts on lip salve

in the movie
about her double life

and I certainly know
what dew is

and how wetness
slides around a hand

The bathmat is off white
almost grey

a bit like something
to feel sad about

something to kneel down on
perhaps pray

Colette Bryce

A Last Post

My ideal job?
Inspector of the tideline,
the ocean's eyebrow,

after the sea
has sucked in its breath
and closed its lashes. I'd live

in a wrecked Bishopean shack,
the lion's paw prints massive
in the sand, and always

in weather like this,
in tattered old shorts
and a vest, my skin salted.

A currency of driftwood
and feathers, necklaces of wrack
like cured leather,

I'd collect in a basket
to barter with the wind.
With shells and fish hooks,

alphabet of bird bone
and twig, I'd fashion
flotsam poems, in my utter

element, pottering along
far from the roar
and heat of politics.

Odd times, a hound
might spring out of nowhere
after a ball, an anoraked owner

in its wake; or I'd wave
to the lone kayaker, buoyant
always as a bath-toy in the waves,

but really, at home
with my own company
I'd be; barely curious enough

to track those trails
of human spoor to the point
at which they always disappear.

Chen Chen

Year's End

I saw my ancestor making omelets

from leftover bits of shadow. I stood up
to give a standing ovation to each now fluffy morsel
of dark. Then I stayed

standing, ovationing every shadow,

including the ancestor's, the houseplant's,
& mine. When I was done, I had a question. *Ancestor*, I said,
am I in a sense your

shadow, or are you somehow mine?

& my ancestor said, *Sure*. & went about
plating the omelets with immense confidence,
though obviously did not know

which was my preferred plate

for omelets. It was then I realized that perhaps
I hadn't given a standing ovation.
Could one person do such a thing?

Or was it only non-seated

clapping? I wanted to ask my ancestor that, but
having sat down by this point,
it was time to eat.

Eiléan Ní Chuilleanáin

Seaweed

for Thomas Dillon and Geraldine Plunkett, married April 23rd, 1916

Everything in the room got in her way,
the table mirror catching the smoke
and the edges of the smashed windowpanes.
Her angle downward on the scene
gave her a view of hats and scattered stones.
She saw her brother come out to help
with the barricades, the wrecked tram
blocking off Earl Street, then back inside.

And for the man in the room, obscured
by her shadow against the window,
the darkening was a storm shifting his life —
he wondered, where were they now, and would
this perch above the scene blow apart soon,
and he imagined the weeds that sink their filaments
between rocks to nourish a life in water
until all of a sudden they're sheared away to sea.

And out at sea the gunboat was bucking and plunging,
throwing up spray. The weeds are slapped
back again on sharp rocks beside beaches
that are sucked bare by the storm after this one,
their holdfast plucked away. He was thinking,
would they find a place and lose it, blown away
again, and find another, on the western coast,
as the seaweed is landed, a darkness in the dark water.

Jane Clarke

Copper Soles

(in memory of Shirley McClure, 1962-2016)

In an old Finnish story
the hero must build a boat from oak

to bear him home through a raging storm
but he cannot complete his work

without three magic words;
the first will secure the stern,

the second will fasten the ledges,
the third will ready the forecastle.

To find the words
he must walk across points of needles,

edges of hatchets,
blades of swords,

for which he needs shoes
with copper soles.

Dear friend,
while the doctors chase pain

around your body,
where will we find such a cobbler?

Cath Drake

Our Front Garden

Every week she stands in our front garden
for at least a few minutes. Her gaze is clouded
but focused: there's nothing disingenuous about it.

She dresses up: shined shoes, lipstick,
a silver brooch clipping together a coat or shawl.
At first we thought she wanted something.

My husband spoke to her several times,
my daughter offered her cake – she didn't
take any notice. We left out a comfortable chair

but she preferred to stand. In the five years
we've been in this house, we've put up a fence,
had a paint job, pulled up the rose garden,

my husband's new truck pitched on the verge,
a tricycle bogged in the herb patch, but nothing
fazed her. We noticed that her red coat

was getting worn then she bought a blue one
with a black collar and matching gloves. Perhaps
coming here was the first time she wore them?

Her gentle humming is a good companion
to my husband's gardening. We look forward
to seeing her, watching her face change

as she steps off the kerb into our garden.
It marks our week. She's been late by a day or two
only a few times – I suspect for good reason.

Out shopping on the high road, I've seen her
on her way to our place and I admit following her
more than once – at a respectful distance.

There's a satisfying labour in her steps
up the steep pavement, across the muddy park.
Strolling behind, I feel a purpose in life

and a little envious. Caught in the traction of my week,
she seems to silence me with her presence so that
I wonder if I've lost my way, should be more

committed to something or dress better.
I'd like to send her a Christmas card,
but I think it's not appropriate. And if one day

she doesn't come, we wouldn't know what to do,
who to tell, how to mark it and our garden
would once again be like anyone's garden.

Paul Farley

Quadrat

After the disaster he went to inspect
a certain patch of rock between the tides.
Oiled guillemots were getting all the headlines,
barrels of ink being spent on their black feathers

while limpets and sea snails went by the by,
the small print of the shoreline. Big surf boomed
and echoed off the stacks. He scratched four corners
to make a window on a glassy mudstone

and started counting what was clinging on there
in summer, when it baked blue at low water,
in winter, when it shone glossy as the ravens
that hijacked one another in the wind,

heading home to tabulate the numbers
in a kitchen where a Rayburn and a storm lamp
provided light and shelter enough for study.
A slow newsroom. The scholar's habitat.

No crossword, horoscope, or game of chess
on the beach with Death, or even noughts and crosses,
just a census of who lives at one address,
what's happening in the constellation Quadrat,

no op-ed column or gastropod gossip
of mantled ears pressed to the world's wall,
just the act of having drawn a line around things
and a willingness to take whatever's found there,

the spill long having sailed the front pages
and dispersed into the archives and the footnotes,
and why he stuck it no one knew, until one day
he handed on his solar paper round

to a poet. Big mistake. I've let things slide.
The data set crumbled while I stayed home
to polish the words. The window washed away.
And that was the last entry, and this is the poem.

Maria Ferguson

My Letters

after Hugo Williams

They are under the bed.
Burning a hole in the carpet again.
I can smell the fabric singe.

Cigarette lit from the hob, eighteen, drunk
on tequila I bought to impress you,
forgot the limes.

Used a Cif synthetic lemon I found in the cupboard
to ease the taste; it's the last thing I remember,
that smell of burning hair.

Some I have kept for almost a decade.
My handwriting has changed a little;
they are tired things and sad.

They long to be held by your fingers,
they want you to understand, but it's been
so long and there are so many now,

these letters I write and do not send.
I think you're meant to throw them away
but I never get that far.

They are hiding under bank statements,
photographs, receipts,
self-destructing, overheating.

I taste it on my tongue, Saxa,
cheap tequila. You sat on my bed
that night, asked me what was burning.

Carolyn Forché

Museum of Stones

These are your stones, assembled in matchbox and tin,
collected from roadside, culvert, and viaduct,
battlefield, threshing floor, basilica, abattoir—
stones, loosened by tanks in the streets,
from a city whose earliest map was drawn in ink on linen,
schoolyard stones in the hand of a corpse,
pebble from Baudelaire's *oui*,
stone of the mind within us
carried from one silence to another,
stone of cromlech and cairn, schist and shale, hornblende,
agate, marble, millstones, ruins of choirs and shipyards,
chalk, marl, mudstone from temples and tombs,
stone from the silvery grass near the scaffold,
stone from the tunnel lined with bones,
lava of a city's entombment, stones
chipped from lighthouse, cell wall, scriptorium,
paving stones from the hands of those who rose against the army,
stones where the bells had fallen, where the bridges were blown,
those that had flown through windows, weighted petitions,
feldspar, rose quartz, blue schist, gneiss, and chert,
fragments of an abbey at dusk, sandstone toe
of a Buddha mortared at Bamian,
stone from the hill of three crosses and a crypt,
from a chimney where storks cried like human children,
stones newly fallen from stars, a stillness of stones, a heart,
altar and boundary stone, marker and vessel, first cast, load and hail,
bridge stones and others to pave and shut up with,
stone apple, stone basil, beech, berry, stone brake,
concretion of the body, as blind as cold as deaf,
all earth a quarry, all life a labor, stone-faced, stone-drunk

with hope that this assemblage of rubble, taken together, would
   become
a shrine or holy place, an ossuary, immovable and sacred
like the stone that marked the path of the sun as it entered the
   human dawn.

Matthew Francis

Ladybird Summer

That summer there was a plague of ladybirds, drifting
    over the garden in a reddish smoke.
        We'd find them on the carpet,
a smattering of coral beads from a broken necklace,
    but self-willed, crawling every which way, mating
        like tiddlywinks.

The flowering season for insects. Crickets twitched the grass,
    moths trundled under their paper-dart wings
        or crouched on the ceiling
in the circle of brighter light above the lampshade,
    and the mosquitoes balanced on the wall
        on moon-lander legs.

Trees split in the heat. We drove through a tawny country
    now turned to outback. In the pub courtyard
        we talked till the colour
drained from the petunias in the hanging baskets,
    unwilling to go home carrying the weight
        of the day's air.

There was too much summer. The ladybirds that gathered
    on ledges to be crunched by the closing windows
        had lost their picture-book brightness.
We were glad of the first sign of autumn, a bowl of plums,
    frost blooming on their skin, and tart sunshine
        in their yellow flesh.

Mina Gorji

The Wasp

who makes no honey gave us ink.
In early spring oak galls appear:
darkening in autumn
they gestate.

Emerging into English light,
this tiny emigrant
was smuggled in Aleppo oak –
an alien acorn.

Lesley Harrison

Thursday Poem

All afternoon, she opens
her eyelids, stretching yellow limbed,
her body slipping water, the lichen's slow explosions spreading

like barnacles. The tide runs through her thighs,
saline and dull, black with eels that slick into her side
where she is frayed like an anemone. It was

like opening a door. The water pressed her down
shoulders first, beneath the cockle shelf where clouds of sperm
seeped through her hair, her muscle tongue
retreating, words fluttering in the sand, digging in.

Now she mouths her own astonished O
at the flood that will wash her clean again: her broken
nails, her still, lovely face full of joy, swallowing.

Michael Haslam

16/2/47

Snow fell from heaven while Aneurin Bevan
thought to spawn the NHS. Mother had drunk
her Guinness bottles on prescription nonetheless.
    Snow fell cold and soft on fold and croft.
Snow fell on Halliwell. Snow drifted into windrow
and an even swell. Snow overwhelmed the mill,
the mine, the railwayline. The world was frozen
in a shell of economic standstill. Snow blown over
Smithills Moor and Winter Hill had heaped against
the hospital, up to the window-sill.
    Such beauty thrills that still receptacle,
the unborn soul, a perfect hole. Snow fills
(rare phrase this for Northern England) Shaly Dingle:
Curl and cornice, turquoise light in ice crevasse.
Each being singularly single and subject
to chimes and tingle, such epiphanies as this'll
once or twice happen have come to pass.
    Snowfall bridges ridge and gable. Snow drifts up
by Hollin Wood. Sub-zero air, a few lights twinkle, but
the power cuts at night. The gate-stoup wind-side ice
withstood. Snow fell on Havercroft and Heaton: White.
    Blue, limply furled, cord-strangled, almost lifeless
as the nurses thump and batter, I was beaten
into breath: At last, some minutes old, I do protest
about my own ejection into this cold world. I'm told
it was a matter, simply, of my life or death.

Seán Hewitt

October

Once, I knelt staring in a garden
in mid-autumn at the last
of the marrow flowers –

a pair pushed up out of nowhere
overnight, too late for the season:
one bent under dew, the frail skin

of the other already turning
slowly back to water.
And yet the leaves bristled

in the wind – the tired petals
not quite ready to give up
to the cold, though each

was a distillation of the sun's
late colour. And I saw myself
kneeling in the garden

from far away, caught between
one man I no longer love,
another I might never.

This is how the world turns:
love like a marrow flower closing,
like another trying still to open.

Selima Hill

Thousands upon Thousands of Beetles

I'm lying on my bed in my bandages
listening to the sounds far below me

of thousands upon thousands of beetles,
returning home from parties, being crushed.

Katherine Horrex

Parliament, Fallen

We can afford to know nothing
beyond concrete, the concatenate
glower of windows.
The street below is a shortcut
for us, though we hate to be dripped on
by clothes horse balconies.

Looking up means a view
through a dark kaleidoscope,
where leaden basslines beat
at the air with all the thunder of hives.
It calls to mind the shuttered
instability of hearts.

As a disused mall this polygon
could be acceptable. Instead
we wonder if there are people
in the hidden parts of the panopticon,
waiting to reveal just how
brittle they've become,

a helter-skelter's skeleton
bleach-stripped by the sun,
the sweet vomit smell of bleach itself,
and we consider
whether something built purely to function
can only fall to ruin,

the city's sirens congregating
in these quads,
where anyone talking talks boldly
in a voice that spreads to fill the space
shaped to keep its own
community of echoes.

Avril Joy

Skomm

Skomm is an old Norse word meaning shame

The girl with the goose on her head sits
by the window in the corner of the classroom,
there are others with her, among them
her sister, their geese barely a wing less visible.
The weight of goose swells the air, the room is ripe
with the scent of goose shit.
I put down my bag, take off my scarf and coat
and wonder about the snow covering the road.
Outside the wind is up and the yard is frosting over.
Better make a start, I say. They pick up pens, open
books. The girl with the goose on her head declines
to write, says she cannot concentrate for the load,
the poundage, shortened neck, compacted spine,
for centuries of carrying: *scamu*, *skomm*, shame,
the bird force fed, gavage-pipe in the oesophagus,
on its back, legs splayed, neck craned, half-buried
in its chest, the words whispered in a father's bed.
She says she cannot stop thinking, *None of us can,*
the nights are the worst,
corralled, wings beating, they leave their bodies,
fly up in a blizzard, a captive murmuration.
Jesus, look at the snow. Will you get home alright
Miss? What about the kids?
I look out at the fattening flakes, the absent ground.
I taste the goose
all twenty pounds of it, sweat and stink.
Snow falls on my tongue the lightest it's been.
I'll get home alright, I say, *now close your books.*
What will it be?
A story, say the girls with geese,
and they fold their arms, lay down their heads.

Peter Kahn

Little Kings

8th Grade. No parents home at Rob Kenton's house.
Six of us watch *Young Frankenstein* in the basement
buzzed on Little Kings Ale. 8 packs of 8-ouncers.

Green bottles, cuddled like teddy bears we hide
in the closet instead of tossing. Commercial
for *Laverne and Shirley*—we toast the TV. Chuckle

and chug. Stand like chorus girls—kick legs, slur,
*5, 6, 7, 8…schmeil, schmazzle, Hoppenstead
incorporated!* No parents, teachers, bullying big brothers.

The movie comes back on. I-Gor's eyes bulging remind
me of my own, beer-blurred. Parents due in an hour,
we take a last gulp of Little Kings. Each of us vow

to finish off an 8-pack. I stop at five—cautious
then, as now, listening to the retching. Six
had Jeff burping, cursing

his big sister—she bought the beer.
Dr. Franken*steen* calls Frau Blücher and horses neigh
and whinny, kicking their rear legs as we clutch our stomachs.

Seven beers made Rob empty his belly like a torn bag
of groceries. Eight got Karl wide-eyed, muttering snot-filled
gibberish as if the real Frankenstein monster, bolts and all,

was stomping his way. Did he see Rob's pale pieced-together
face waxy from the mortician three years later after riding shotgun
to a drunken Cuervo Gold driver?

The doorbell rings repeatedly—drawing us from
our subterranean castle. Reminding us we were all fuzzy
mustache and puff of bony chest we hoped made us look old

enough to buy our own beer. Three years later, in the funeral parlour
it's clear our crowns were from Burger King. Our kingdom,
youth's puffed up buzz.

Simon Lewis

Circle Time

You were sat beside me listening
to the others — the gas lad telling joke
after joke about boys in the townland,
two bucks on the edge of the circle
debating the merits of a Passat
over a Škoda. We sit together

at every family party; we shake hands
and you tell me I'm getting younger
and you laugh, patting yourself
on your bald head, slapping me on the back.
I ask about the farm but you're yearning
for a proper chat about tractors,

baling techniques, the best value cattle feed.
A farm is not what you talk about with me.
City rearing has no currency here
in this place, where acreage is king,
so you stand, trudge to another chair and start
laughing, shaking hands, slapping backs.

Fran Lock

On insomnia

And contemplate this: the heat-treated hairdos of next door
neighbours, the roseate nosebleeds of fuckboys in hoodies;
your own face, rinsed in the mirror, the sweet green sweat
you're riddled with in mornings, a rock pool reflection under
algaecidal light. You are going nowhere. This poem yokes
you, to the pain you are chronic and adipose with; to the desk,
to the chair, to ergonomic purgatory. And to the body, its
spasms and its rhapsodies, three part harmonies, one chord
wonders. *You will never be whole.* The voices. His voice,
broadcast on your remedial frequency, making its way
through a rubbishy dusk, the streetlamps beaming fizzy glow
like Lucozade. You will never be whole. Vomit o'clock
and the brain is Kraken, white and shaking. Open the window,
pry the chipboard from the window; fill your punctured eye
with stars. And contemplate this: Saturday night and the dirt
purrs with it; cars, litter bins, pit bull dogs. A girl with high
Yorick cheekbones drags a false nail down the scratchy
surface of a bri-nylon sleeplessness. A man rides ignorance
like a white horse, kicking mirrors from parked cars. You
have the itch under your skin. Insectile dysfunction. Lust,
with its own murky gravities. *You will fail.* You have not
made a friend of this city and *you will fail.* Cup your eyes
like coins. Addiction holds such simplicity. Check your
used-car contours in the broken glass. You are going
nowhere. They cannot nail you to a pronoun, hot mess
of cravings and behaviours, tainted frailty, old meat's
rancid rainbow. Ugly. Contemplate. Consider: your
lilies, toiling like deaf ears, tearing the tired night a new
one, stirring a sulphate dust in your veins. Your eyes
are blue with pseudo-scientific toxicity, with chemical
expectancy, a dread that dries a smile like paint. Your
blood is on fire, full of bellicose adrenaline, nitrate

and neon; brighter, even, than the hoary fluorescence
of angels. It is so late. And you are pining the rhinestone
shine of a lost narcotism. Now trauma's your ergotamine.
Trauma, your ergot, your argot of rye. Awful thought
that treads the brain's rank breadth. Silence. Pray silence.
Pray the dark room away, the candles, the pious vibrations
of flame; the dim bulb with its gospel of moths, one
hundred pairs of gloved hands clasped to powder.
Marooned in your gooseflesh, one hand does not know
what the other is doing. It's three a.m. the mind's alive
like frostbite, a cold burn that blackens things. Your
graphite smile could shatter. Thoughts of him have
poisoned you, rust in the blood. You have not eaten
for days, you mottle, run your own hands over your
oxidising thighs, watch the bruises ripen to a landmass,
a landmark, a *brave new world*, a *here be dragons*.
You listen to yourself, creaking like rope; your body, its
canned laughter repeating mean and low, throwing
out thought according to the malnourished algorithm
some devil has devised. You clutch and sway in a crêpe
air and you *want-want-want* what you'll never have
again: sleep; his image breaking across your scrubbed
flesh like surf. Contemplate this: this is forever.
There is no movie montage where you'll shop yourself
to transformation. You will never be whole. And grief
is not a line we walk to wellness; the tidy smirk
of therapy, the therapised, the girls licking flakes of gold
leaf pastry from a Pret a Manger croissant, saying *you
should take up yoga*. Grief is a longing in the body, your
body, the machine-tooled aesthetics of starvation. It's
so uncool, a super-terrestrial emptiness; the acetone eroded
teeth of your disorder. He will not come again. Sleep will
not come, and make an amnesty of bandages, the white
ribbons rendering you prematurely maypole. It will not
wrap you. It will not keep you. It will not launder or
succour you. It will break into your ballerina box, will

chew the jewels from their semi-precious sockets, set
them pulsing in your frontal lobe. Your heart has
a headache. Drink raw egg. Or Dettol. It's up to you.
The sky is pasteurised by thunder...

Ed Madden

A Pooka in Arkansas

My dad was dying. He had been dying
for weeks. I went for a walk down
the old road beside the family home,
the sun declining in the distant trees.
Be careful, my mother said, there are wolves
in the fields—she said she had seen the tracks.
I used the walk to phone my love back home,
the man they didn't know, refused to know,
a name they never used. The nearest field
was fringed with what the combines left behind
of last year's harvest, threaded now with insects
and weeds. Tractors would plow it all down
soon enough, and death would be here, too,
soon. On the road ahead, a small dog
trotted just beyond me. The wind picked up,
I tucked my phone away. No one headed
out or home, no one on the road,
just the dog. It paused, looked back as if
to ask, how far do you think we'll go tonight

Nick Makoha

They Will Call This Evidence

The river from the night before functioned as an eye
in twilight when the true causes were removed from sight.
The naming of things and their actions had also disappeared.
All we had at our disposal were the outlines of suffering;
a house waiting for a boy who would not return, his body
leaking heat to a stubborn wind demanding to be heard
and a version of night I had not seen before. Who knows
what running water thinks or its afterthoughts? By the forest
when the wolf walked out, I was certain we too were prey.
But the function of the eye in this world is to draw whatever
is placed in front of it. A rotor blade, midges, boredom
and its power of invention. How else can an evening
in its own darkness present a boy's body at rest? Are ghosts
a sign of a hurried life? The flesh in search of its own interior.

Rachel Mann

Book of Jonah

Somewhere beneath the dry blast of sun:
Jones. D, David, Dai, Jonah –
Nineveh's boy-prophet.

In his pack, hard tack and stencils, the loneliness
Of words, vials of the Blood,
And haunch of Holy Lamb –

Behold, he comes, Jonah-bach,
Behold, reluctantly, to engrave a century –
Cry out, saith the Lord.

Out of the belly of Sheol, he draws spitsticker
And scorper, dead men ever-near,
He draws out sharpening-stone,

He cuts wounds in wood,
He sings: dead men feel no fear, dead men,
Their greatcoats hold promises deep –

He too has needs: of sleep, of dreams,
Of Pellam, the Lady of the Pool, his tools
Carve: *Repent of thy wickedness. Begin!*

Mary McCollum

the boy with dark eyes

a rose and a broken vase

water spilling
finding its way through the cracks
of the scrubbed wooden table

light reflecting from the surface

the boy with dark eyes looks straight through you

the past has nothing to do with him

he lives without memory
in the rinsed bowl of the present

the tap permanently running

Shane McCrae

The Hastily Assembled Angel on Care and Vitality

The hastily assembled angel watches
From the air he watches   from that point in the air
Where years from now the apex of the pyra-
mid he is watching being   built will be
Invisibly   he watches as slaves roll
Huge stones from the quarry to the pyramid the
Slave who invented   the method for moving
The stones is dead   the stones   that were too big
For human beings to move   the angel saw
The slave was killed for   attempting to correct
The implementation of his method   which
The Egyptian engineers had not at first
Completely understood   though even as
His dark blood made the dirt beside them dark
They saw the first board buckle   beneath the weight
Of the first stone   fortunately the slave had
Explained his method often to his fellow
Slaves   and they could when they were ordered to
Silently make it work the angel sees the
Slaves serve their masters most   efficiently
When they aren't talking to each other   but
They serve their masters most   quickly just after
They have devised a plan to kill their masters

Momtaza Mehri

Haematology #2

This is the age of nightly nosebleeds. You are indecently abundant.
There is a conceptual gap between your thighs. Pillowcases moult
    faster than election promises.
You mourn each darling erythrocyte's sink into whirlpools –
into the lonely hours, into the heartlands of bin liners. They
    don't know what to do with you.

Stay with you. Take this shedding as a sign of what's to come. *This*
    country is slowly killing us.
She says this & you bite your lip. *That's what you said the last time*
    about that other place –
& the place before that & the place before that. Funny that. The host
    destroying the parasite.
This dunya got cruel jokes for days. For days & days & oh the nights.
    The back ends of the *back homes.*

Sticky, tea-stained nights. The houseboy would serve us chopped
    liver & lemonade.
The sides of the glass as wet as the rims of his eyes. You almost
    hear the syrup of his heartache.
Its throaty, tubular descent. He belongs to a lesser tribe. You
    don't know what that means yet.
Only that the youngers call him boy. Call him something other
    than his name.

You know him not by name, but by blood. By the sleight of hand
    we call luck.
By the membrane dividing your life, your delusions, from his.
    You blot from the inside out.
History is a hangnail we take turns picking at. *This country is*
    slowly killing us.
You think he could be talking about this place. He could be
    talking about anywhere.

Abegail Morley

Barometer

After the funeral words
were deadpan, slipped
down my throat like gullied-rain.
Today the weather's changed,
someone's placed graph paper
against the pane, plotted the day –
it peaks around ten.

I snake out of sheets,
abandon them like a swag of leaves,
move across the room
with the slow precision
of newly-oiled machinery.

Paul Muldoon

Corncrake and Curlew

The corncrake marvels at the land being green
although the winter's harsh.
The curlew knows the land's so green
because it's mostly marsh

rendered by a few broad strokes
of a palette knife
and the merest whiff of tents, wood smoke,
a red jacket, drums and fifes.

This same corncrake once hitched its star
to a horse-drawn reaper.
The curlew, meanwhile, has ranged so far
it's now been issued with a beeper.

The corncrake ratchets up the odds
of being cut down in the aftermath.
The curlew has followed an execution squad
along this muddy path

to the telephone pole
that's still smeared
with creosote-blood and the bog hole
into which the body's disappeared.

The corncrake sounds but one alarm.
Faithless, fickle,
the curlew moves from big farm to big farm
with its little scythe or sickle

to oversee pig killing, the shearing of sheep,
the combine's thrum and strum.
Its lonesome wheep's
a counterpoint to fife and drum.

The corncrake's oblivious to its rasp
catching a sentry off guard.
The curlew's come to grasp
the idea that running a credit card

across a fine-tooth comb
is a surefire corncrake summons.
From its observation dome
the curlew has long since taken in the comings

and goings of little platoons
filing off three-mast ships
and hauling to lorries parked beyond the dunes
crates of rifles and rifle clips.

The corncrake marvels at the land being green
although the hay's been saved.
The curlew knows the land's so green
because it's a mass grave.

Sharon Olds

Departure Gate Aria

She was standing near a departure gate,
sandal-footed, her wiggly hair
and the latticework of her mercury footwear
the same satiny gold, and there was something
wistful about her, under the burnish
of her makeup she looked extremely young,
and a little afraid. I wanted to speak
to her, as if I were a guardian spirit
working the airport – God knows
I was crazed with my fresh solitariness –
so I did a little double take,
when I passed her, and said, Could I ask, where did you
get your sandals – my husband, I lied,
wants me to get some, and she said a name, as if
relieved to speak. Thanks, I said,
they look great with your hair – actually
(my head bowed down on its own), you look
like a goddess. Her face came out from behind
its cloud, You don't know how I needed that!,
she cried out, I'm going to meet my boyfriend's
parents. You'll do just fine, I said, you look
beautiful and good. She looked joyful. I bustled off –
so this is what I'll do, now,
instead of kissing and being kissed, I'll
go through airports praising people, like an
Antichrist saying, You do not need
to change your life.

Roberto Pastore

Just So You Know

I'm on my way over
in my favourite blue pyjamas
to rip that novel from your head.

Don Paterson

Death

His trick – by which I mean the way he'd convince you of his
earnestness –
was to actualise at some random and unpredictable post,
unruffled, immaculate,
like he'd been there all along: vaping at the turn of the stairs,
taking a leak in the adjacent stall,
or turning round from the seat in front in the empty matinee,
saying *C'mon. We've been through this.*
And again I'd get up and leave, and mutter *I'm not ready yet,*
and he'd say
OK bud, see you tonight, knowing we all got worn down by
this in the end.

Before they kicked me upstairs, I used to work in sales. I still
have a case of free samples
and an eye for an easy mark. One day, he was working
through some genre clichés
to keep himself amused, and I was closing the bathroom
cabinet when I saw him at my shoulder.
I shrieked, he cracked up laughing; I swung round, and we fell
into the usual threadbare exchange.
But I caught him running the back of his hand across my
pima cotton towels
and sneak a sidelong look at my new sonic toothbrush, with
more than just a casual interest;
I noticed his Prada suit was a size too large, and his floral tea
cologne was Tommy Girl
though it smelled pretty good on him. It was then I really saw
it. His weakness.
I said *Look, look – I'll do you a deal. No deals,* he says. *You
know that. Hear me out,* I say. *It's legit.*
*Give me another twenty years, and I'll kit you out. I'll be your
go-to guy. I'm serious. Knockdown rates.*

He said nothing, but the sweat was forming on his upper lip
and brow.
So I got out the case and did my old routine, told him I'm
practically giving this stuff away;
though it was tough to see him so easily played, so easily
reduced, so worried and frantic –
me pulling out one thing after another, him suddenly
wondering if he could afford it all,
patting his pockets, wondering if I took plastic, wondering if
he *had* plastic,
what plastic even was – his arms full of all the cool new things
he wanted,
a black fedora, a snakeskin belt, the silk tie with the Mondrian
design, but then realising
that he was technically neither salaried nor self-employed –
a slave to his work, he'd always thought,
but really just a slave, hand-to-mouth, hardly ever in the same
town two nights in a row,
sleeping on couches between gigs, everything he wore lifted
from the closets of the dead,
everything he ate, whatever the dead had left uneaten on the
stove after he'd walked them to the car.
All he wanted was a night off, a table at Clio's so he could
work through the card,
and then to go home to his own shit – some old jazz on vinyl,
a valve amplifier,
a good espresso machine and a workout bike, and maybe a
wife and kids too, in time,
but whenever he thought of them, or rather what they'd talk
about round the big TV,
the kitchen table as he made his famous chilli, or the school
gate after hockey practice –
all he could ever think of was him delivering the bad news as
usual, the worst.
'Daddy, what do you mean *I must leave with you now?*'

Don't think for a second that Death loves his work. Even
    though I couldn't stop –
we both knew there was no way he could pay for any of this
    stuff – I was holding back the tears for him:
who wants to see their own death fall to such a two-bit hustle?
    In the end I gave up. I hugged him. I said
*It's OK, it's OK. I'll go with you. Just give me five to get some
    things and say goodbye to folks.*
And he was fine with that, and so innocently grateful when I
    really did come back, carrying a near-new pair of brogues,
a couple of good shirts and a nice blue jacket that I reckoned
    would fit him well,
and I could see in his eyes that over the years he'd lost more
    than a few of us this way,
to this old play, and each of us had cost him like a life.

David Pollard

1543

He who, with care, saved the appearances,
whose guiding hand had never lost its touch
defraying all its losses on the dimensions
God had granted, touched up
the dolorosas of the court
whose eyes had played with danger
and the pretence of home, lips, prayers;
followed Vesalius, master of the real,
trusted the evidence of each finger's
whorl as it brushed against the blood
and flesh of the old gods, prophesying
mortality like the plucked lute
and virginalls.

He sang them, gentle, onto canvas,
held down their souls so
they could see the same old sun
filtered through the veins' last knowing,
showed how in a quick brush with
likeness, semblance can lie
yet is our only hope.

Until the year the earth moved –
rode the Copernican aether from its
centre of the *orbium coelestium* to
its dry outer edge where it could
wither into mortality with all the other
orbs of rust around the heavens.

In that year, in a side street and alone,
knotted about with silence
in the last distant orbit
of his trammels
died Holbein,
away from all the centres of
the painted tricks of power.
There, his *corporis fabrica*
drew in its horns
in a plague year.

Michael Rosen

Raspberry Pip

All hail to the raspberry pip, survivor, desperate to
stick between the teeth; wedge itself like a pebble in
a tyre-tread; it refuses to be dissolved or shrunk,
it hunkers down, cornered, resisting a poking with
your finger-nail, and even the tooth-pick can fail.

All hail to the raspberry pip, hiding in its scarlet globule,
migrating into your mouth, a bird's beak, a fox's jaw,
disguised as softness, waiting to be munched, ready
for the peristalsis, the long slide through.

All hail to the raspberry pip, heading for a spot of dirt, a
railway siding, where it becomes a bramble, winding and
arching its thorny way, obstreperous enough to delay
your longing for the fruit until it has fully scarletted.

Julie-ann Rowell

Fata Morgana

The world turns upside down
the lighthouse lies flat on its back
houses swap position
high now low, hills swoon in pink
old stone cross flipped
the fisherman fidgets, blinks

          Island restores itself
like a flipped coin
tail to head, head to tail again
the sea ironed black
land straightened with a shudder
dizzy from its exercise
the fisherman all buttoned up

Fiona Sampson

Mother as Eurydice

Suddenly I want to call
out to her
a slim girl (it seems)
(but she flickers)
to call her up

like a blue
flame
(she might blow out)
flickering in the doorway
of my first memory

she was beautiful
in ways impossible
to understand
not her bones face hair
or all of these

flickering because I was half-asleep
        because film judders
in the yellow doorway
of early memory
before the words come in

her gaze was
a blue
burning gasp
terrifying   perfect   gone

Tom Sastry

A man's house catches fire

I was suddenly uncomfortably hot
but I have always had these surges, and at first
I thought the smell of smoke
was just me going off my head

which I have learnt to expect.
I closed the curtains, undressed
turned the heating off and lay
in the last of my stillness

watching the shadow of a flame
playing on the wall
until the shadow reddened
and I could see no way out.

It's been a month now
with the fire still raging
and me not dead
and no help coming

so today I stepped outside
smelling more than ever of myself.
My oldest friend was passing.
She said *Is it that time?*

Are the houses of men burning too?
I said *You're mistaken.*
Nothing is burning.
and I stepped back into my house.

Seni Seneviratne

Dear Dad

Does this seem odd? This replying to letters
sent, all those years ago, from a troopship?

What with me not due to be born for another
ten years and you dead now, this past thirty.

No matter. I know you, at least, believed in
an afterlife, so I'll hope you are receiving me.

That reference to your trip on the *Orama*
from Ceylon to England twelve years ago

makes me sorry I never asked you more
about that crossing as well as this one.

How optimistic you sound – that familiar
"glass half-full" attitude you always had.

One hundred and forty-eight men squeezed
into cramped mess quarters to eat and sleep,

and you're writing about how the hammock's
comfortable enough for a good night's rest.

It's so typical of you to think of going up on deck
when rough seas made the mess unbearable.

Wrapped up in your greatcoat and balaclava,
did you watch the stars until you fell asleep?

I'll write more soon. This is just a short note
to say, wherever you are, I am thinking of you.

Penelope Shuttle

Noah's Arche, Day One Hundred

As the wateriness of the world continued
supplies of Armenian apples got lower.

Spiders studied their Breviaries of Health
full of old English advice

while the supersaliency of the rutting elephants
set the boat a'rocking.

The wolf-greyhound nipped Noah's ankle,
the best philosophy that wise beast knew.

The weasel practised her fine court-hand.
The night-raven was on tenterhooks all the time

but everyone spoilt the little lamb.

The rain hung its pearly garlands everywhere
as if for a young girl's funeral.

The snail crept over his delightfully-illustrated prayer book.
The Arche ploughed on like Leander.

Men of Troy, said the circling whale, trust not in The Horse.

Noah's wife had a rose cheek.
Her sons were favoured into Latin by the alchemists.

The dilling pig coughed quietly in his stinky pen
and the rabbits gave up democracy in favour of government by
    demons.

The bear sported a half-moon eye patch.
The lark enjoyed a gobbet-royal.

A dreamy louse raised Hymen's torch.
The sloths did almost nothing at all.

The lioness roared her lore spell
and the paradise tree-snake took notes (kind-of).

All day Noah gazed out over the Marinorama.
Oh to be mocked by a mermaid! To know the colour of her keen
    eyes!

In that Arche three hundred cubits long
no creature could abide the half-wit polecat.

And the name of Noah's mother?
Unrecorded.

Danez Smith

my president

today, i elect jonathan, eleven & already making roads out of water
young genius, blog writer, lil community activist, curls tight
as pinky swears, black as my nation   i trust the world in his tender
blooming hands, i trust him to tell us which rivers are safe to drink
& which hold fish like a promise

    & i elect eve ewing, who i know would ms. frizzle the country
    into one big classroom where grandmas finger paint
    the national budget & uncles stand around smoking blacks
    plotting on stars for our escape   she could walk to the podium
    at her inauguration & say, *the future is now*, & we'd all marvel
    at the sun & moon looping the sky like a gif as the cars learned
    to fly & our skin grew bulletproof

& colin kaepernick is my president, who kneels on the air
bent toward a branch, throwing apples down to the children & vets

    & rihanna is my president, walking out of global summits
    with wineglass in hand, our taxes returned in gold
    to dust our faces into coins

& my mama is my president, her grace stunts
on amazing, brown hands breaking brown bread over
mouths of the hungry until there are none unfed

    & my grandma is my president & her cabinet is her cabinet
    cause she knows to trust what the pan knows
    how the skillet wins the war

    & the man i saw high kicking his way down the river?
    he is my president

& the trans girl making songs in her closet, spinning the dark
into a booming dress? she too is my president

& shonda rhimes is my president

          & nate marshall is my president

     & trina is my president

   & the boys outside walgreens selling candy
   for a possibly fictional basketball team are my presidents

   & the bus driver who stops after you yell *wait!* only twice
   is my pres

& the dude at the pizza spot who will give you a free slice
if you are down to wait for him to finish the day's fourth prayer
is my president

& my auntie, only a few months clean, but clean
she is my president

     & my neighbor who holds the door open when my arms
     are full of laundry is my president

& every head nod is my president

   & every child singing summer with a red sweet tongue
   is my president

& the birds

      & the cooks

  & the single moms especially

     & the weed dealers

& the teachers

  & the meter maid who lets you slide

& the cab drivers who stop

 & the nurse's swollen feet
& the braider's exhausted hands

  & the bartender
& beyoncé
& all her kids
  & the rabbi

& the sad girls

 & the leather daddy who always stops to say *good morning*

& the boy crying on the train & the sudden abuela who rubs his
 back
& the uncle who offers him water & the drag queen who begins
 to hum

   o my presidents!
   my presidents!
   my presidents!
   my presidents!

 show me to our nation
my only border is my body

   i sing your names
   sing your names
    your names

   my mighty anthem

Julian Stannard

Trolley Man

When someone asks, Could I have
a sandwich with some cheese in it?
I will say No sandwiches today!

And if anyone should ask for coffee
I will say, Hot water not working.
Shocking, isn't it?

I will wheel my trolley from one end
of the train to the other, smiling
magnificently at everyone.

And when a lady asks,
I don't suppose you've got
a piece of shortbread
some lovely, lovely shortbread?

I will say, No my dear
all the lovely shortbread has gone.

Phoebe Stuckes

Fox

I'm usually hanging around
in dressing gowns.
Buttering toast and calling a friend
to complain about poetry
or the government.

It's a rough time to be young
or to care about anything.
So I keep wandering through London
looking for something to do.

I rattle around these streets
like an urban fox.
In my second-hand fur
eating junk out of polystyrene.

I don't like to follow
the thick grey artery that leads
to my flat, where I live with myself.
I tell myself that crying in cabs

could be glamorous
if I did it correctly.
I am doing my best
with bad nights and bad love.
Honey it's difficult.

Maria Taylor

Loop

Maybe time moves like a figure of eight,
surging forwards then back on itself.

Light returns from exploded stars.
A grown woman could turn a corner
and see herself crying as a girl.

Newsflash: our world ends again.
The disappearing forests of childhood
disappear again.

> The path curves.

It takes the woman back to a dimly-lit bar
where she meets the same lover again and again.
She risks everything once more.

They've already met
before they've said a word.

Marvin Thompson

Whilst Searching for Anansi with my Mixed Race Children in the Blaen Bran Community Woodland

I

A fox lies still by a birch. 'Dad, is it dead?'
asks Derys. Crouching down, I watch an ant
crawl through its ear-fur. Inside my head

are Mark Duggan's smile and last night's heavy dread:
I dreamt his death again. A distant love
once stroked my cheek and said: *'They shot him dead*

only because he had a gun.' I still see red
and white carnations; a girl who now frequents
her father's grave; brown birch leaves descending

a walk to school. '85. Mum's palm bled
sweat, Tottenham's air strangely grey. Stagnant.
We passed my friend's burnt front door – flames had fed

on parked cars. In tower blocks, rage had spread
like an Arab Spring: numbing unemployment,
the oppressive use of sus laws. *'Is my friend dead?'*

Mum answered with silence. Hunkered on mud,
my prayer withers, the birch's leaves hang slant
and noonlight shrouds the fox. 'Sorry. It's dead.'
'It's breathing, Dad,' shouts Hayden. 'Listen, hard!'

Crouched by the fox's nose, I listen
to placate my son. The fox is breathing.
Should I leave it here to die? Its fur glistens

with drizzle – each breath makes my eyes moisten
as though a gospel singer's voice is rising
from the fox's lungs. Derys blurts, 'Dad, listen,

it needs a vet!' In the dream, Mark Duggan
lay on the Gold Coast's shore, smoke soaring
above ancestors whose dark necks glistened,

chains ready on docked ships from London.
I woke, limbs tensed, ancestors' rage jumping
in my blood, the humid night laden

with sailors' screams: *'Masts ablaze!'* Will Britain
learn to love my children's melanin?
With their voices ('Yellow bird, high up…') swelling,

I carry the limp fox. The grey mountains
are watching us. A buzzard's circling.

I scratch and scratch my wrists. The vet stiffens,
holding her stethoscope. The fox's eyes listen.

Jack Underwood

Behind the Face of Great White Shark

Glass of water in the dawn kitchen.
Since we brought you home from the hospital
I have begged these hours to a stub.
Please water. Please glass. Great White Shark
always sniffing out the small far blood
and all my murders and funerals out
for revision, mind circling the short grass
like a bored dog on its tether. *Keep your shit
together* picturing a perfect pentagon
freehand, or fucking ambidextrously,
anything to blot the rat-gnawed forehead,
worms correlating, dark target areas.
Two weeks since the last Great White attack
and cowardy custard, in with the green beans,
are you struggling? I admit I have been sick
since we met, pursuing this love-wound
like a moon beyond the windscreen.
Morning leans across us like the shadow
of a closing door. It's not your fault.
Eat your banana. I can keep you safe inland.
I can love you like an expert: my adamant
hands, the voice I lower and lighten,
my arm hair so alert, as the shark turns
its face again, no aspect to discern, no
inclination or decision, just you reaching
both arms up, distracting from the scent,
the plume, the lesser work of living.

Jennifer Wong

of butterflies

Zhuang Zi said
the man does not know

if he dreams of a butterfly
or if the butterfly dreams

of a man. It is unclear
who awakens first   or from where.

Neither do I
know   after all these years

if I am a Chinese girl who
wanted to go home

or a woman from Hong Kong
who will stay in England.

It's British summer time
in my living room

but my watch in the drawer
moves seven hours ahead.

The past: is the door still open?
The future: am I a filial daughter,

living so far away from my parents?
Wearing her marmalade camouflage,

the butterfly of unknowing
pollinates in one world   and another.

Tamar Yoseloff

The Black Place

after Georgia O'Keeffe

How simply she shows us:
a sweep of the brush, her thin wrist
distilling the spring desert
into shades of ruby and gold.

Is there a black line defining
the yellow, or is it just a trick
of contrast? I see it in this *real* sky,
this *real* ridge, the picture I make

with my eyes, the here and now
of sight. She called it 'The Black Place',
perhaps that's why I want to find
that line, to clarify her phrase;

she was in the desert, high noon,
not a trace of cloud. She pulls my eye
to a darker passage, a depression
shadowed in broad light.

When I look up to the sky
in this real place, where the sun
fires my skin, I see a hill behind a hill,
and then another and another:

the place beyond our vision, the place
inside the cave, where the sun
can never reach. It chills me
just to think it into being.

We'll never find it; as soon as we arrive,
the distance shifts to somewhere else,
we remain in foreground, everything moving
around us, even when we're still.

She found the bellow in a skull,
the swagger in a flower; in turn
her lover made her wrist, her breast
his subject. They lived,

exposed their lives to light, and now
they're gone. The black place she made
remains. She shows me how to find it
here, beyond the ridge.

Biographies of the shortlisted writers

Forward Prize for Best Collection

Caroline Bird (b. 1986 Leeds) intended the title of her collection *The Air Year* to refer to the first year of a relationship, 'the anniversary prior to paper / for which ephemeral gifts are traditional'; in the year of coronavirus, it has taken on an eerie double meaning.

She writes: 'I'm fascinated with the idea that poetry is about inserting a mystery into the reader's life not clarifying one, that by the end of a poem you should know less than you did when you started, that a poem is a kind of amnesia injection that makes the immediate world strange again.'

Bird's previous collection, *In These Days of Prohibition*, was shortlisted for both the TS Eliot Prize and the Ted Hughes Award; she is also a playwright, whose credits include *The Trial of Dennis the Menace* and a new version of *The Trojan Women*.

Natalie Diaz (b. 1978 Needles, California, USA) is the holder of a MacArthur 'genius' award, a former professional basketball player and one of the few remaining speakers of the Mojave language. 'Where we come from, we say language has an energy, and I feel that it is a very physical energy.' Diaz's US publishers, Graywolf, describe *Postcolonial Love Poem* as 'an anthem of desire against erasure', of which the erasure of language is just one form.

'Ash can make you clean, / as alkaline as it is a grief', writes Diaz in 'That Which Cannot be Stilled'. Her new collection performs that work of cleansing and mourning, shot through with desire and celebration. 'In this book,' writes Diaz, 'I demanded a different visibility, one that makes my nation uncomfortable – my speakers refused to be defined by their wounds and would instead sow them and reap light from them.'

Vicki Feaver (b. 1943 Nottingham) stole a copy of Blake's poems from her parents' bookshelf as a child and, reading it in bed by torchlight, developed a secret ambition to become a poet. Much of that early encounter went into *I Want! I Want!* – the title is from Blake's engraving, showing a child clambering towards the moon on a ladder, and speaks to Feaver's themes of female ambition and desire. The sections of the book are separated by ladder motifs; Feaver describes testing her editor's patience by insisting 'they were drawn with just the right degree of wobbliness'.

A new collection from Feaver is a rare event; this is only her fourth in 40 years. A poem from her 1993 collection, *The Handless Maiden*, won the Forward Prize for Best Single Poem. She is an emeritus professor at University College, Chichester.

David Morley (b. 1964 Blackpool) writes to give a voice to the voiceless or spoken-over: the British 'Gypsy King' boxer Tyson Fury (the source of his collection's title, *FURY*); the midges at Innominate Tarn; the evicted traveller communities at Dale Farm. Many poems feature words of Angloromani, the mixed language spoken by British Romany; their anger is tempered by a sense of joy in the vast potentialities of speech and oral tradition.

Morley grew up with a stammer, which he has described as a 'merciless muse'. 'My teenage mind developed into a thesaurus of tensioned, alert possibility: hundreds of synonyms and antonyms allowed me to find the path of least resistance through sentences.'

Morley's selected poems, *The Invisible Gift*, won the 2015 Ted Hughes Award.

Pascale Petit (b. 1953 Paris, France) was converted to poetry aged 16, when her teacher recited Keats' 'Ode to a Nightingale'. Her subsequent years as a sculptor and artist allowed her to develop connections between poetry and the visual and tactile. But her aim remained the same, like Keats, 'to create a forest the reader could walk into and see and hear even in the dark'.

Tiger Girl is a departure for Petit. Her imaginative landscapes have shifted from the Amazon rainforest, which characterised earlier collections including *Fauverie* and *Mama Amazonica*, to the forests of Ranthambore in Rajasthan, near her grandmother's birthplace, beautiful and full of life but threatened by poaching, deforestation and climate change. She draws attention to 'how our endangered wild is endangering all life on the planet including ourselves', while leaving room for a sense of awe and astonishment: 'How can we destroy such wonders?'

Felix Dennis Prize for Best First Collection

Ella Frears (b. 1991 Truro) has been poet-in-residence on the number 17 bus in Southampton, at Tate St. Ives, and in a university physics department, among other places. She has written extensively about motorway service stations. These very different subject matters find coherence in Frears' idiosyncratic voice, sense of humour and strange connection-making. Poetic form, for Frears, is unstable and shifty, a way of drawing different registers of language into unexpected collisions.

The heart of *Shine, Darling* is the unsettling long piece 'Passivity, Electricity, Acclivity', detailing an autobiographical near-abduction experience. Interwoven voices and shifting time-frames build up like evidence. 'I wanted to write a long-form lyric poem the length and weight of a short story, with the suspense of a novel,' writes Frears.

Will Harris (b. 1989 London) was shortlisted for the Forward Prize for Best Single Poem in 2018. The poem, 'SAY', is one of the centrepieces of *RENDANG*, drawing together many of Harris's concerns: family, borders, transience, the need for 'a voice capacious enough to be both me and not-me / while always clearly being me'. (He has written elsewhere, in the long essay *Mixed-Race Superman*, that 'the mixed-race person grows up to see the self as something strange and shifting'.)

Writing on *RENDANG* in the *Guardian*, Joanna Lee has described how it 'leans into a vocabulary all of its own, and announces itself as an artefact that will not be dislodged'; a good metaphor for the way Harris's poems frequently build themselves around some undislodged irritation, like the grain of sand which produces a pearl. In 2019, Harris received a Poetry Fellowship from the Arts Foundation.

Rachel Long (b. 1988 London) is the founder of Octavia Poetry Collective for Womxn of Colour, based at Southbank Centre. She began writing poetry after attending a workshop with Jean 'Binta' Breeze, a transformative experience she describes as 'radically intimate, and yet simultaneously expansive. I've been writing poems since I left that room.'

Long writes on love, the family, sexual politics – broad subjects, treated with a pin-sharp attention to the local and specific (an estate 'built like Tetris', the 'lit throat of a candle'). Her advice for poets starting out is to 'listen to the poems more than the noise around you; find good teachers, honour them, make good friends, create a space for yourself and for them'.

Nina Mingya Powles (b. 1993 Wellington, NZ) sees *Magnolia*, 木蘭 as 'partly a collection of love letters to Shanghai, but it's also about loneliness, and about trying to retrace your steps back towards a language you've lost'. (木蘭, 'Mùlán', is the Chinese word for magnolia, the official flower of Shanghai.)

Powles is drawn to writers who treat the boundaries of genre as fluid and permeable. She has described how she prizes the moment when 'something within the line of the poem slips, gives way, and we are pulled suddenly into a different field of language': an excellent description of the experience of reading *Magnolia*, 木蘭. She is currently working on a book of essays about bodies of water, food, migration and being mixed-race, to be published by Canongate in 2021.

Martha Sprackland (b. 1988 Barnstaple) was six when she met her future publisher, Deryn Rees-Jones, at a poetry workshop for children in Sefton Park. (She wrote a poem about a mouse, on purple sugar-paper, with a felt-tip pen.) She works as poetry editor at *Poetry London*, and in 2017 she co-founded her own small press, Offord Road Books, and so is represented in this year's shortlists in all three capacities – editor (of Fiona Benson), publisher (of Ella Frears) and poet.

The poems in *Citadel* enter into a dialogue with the sixteenth-century Queen of Spain, Juana of Castile. Sprackland, who spent a year teaching in Madrid, has described the book as 'a rupture or portal in time, through which two women separated by hundreds of years could talk'. Juana, often known as Juana la Loca, or 'the mad', spent most of her life imprisoned at Tordesillas, the 'citadel' which gives the book its title. 'I wanted to create a different reality in which she could be written to, entertained by a sequence of letrillas, spoken to, kept company.' Sprackland's poems are simultaneously intimate and eerie, circling round motifs of teeth and blood and eggs.

Forward Prize for Best Single Poem

Fiona Benson (b. 1978 Wroughton) won the Forward Prize for Best Collection in 2019, with *Vertigo & Ghost*. 'Mama Cockroach, I Love You' playfully extends some of the themes which characterised the second half of that book: motherhood, acts of caring, vulnerable bodies, 'all the liquors and gravy / of the obscene world'.

The poem is part of an online 'audio pamphlet' about insects, which combines interviews with scientists, Benson's poetry and innovative sound design. She is also working on some poems about school, and poems drawing on the myths of Europa, Pasiphaë and Crete. 'Perhaps, for myself, I want to write more towards the light, more towards gratitude for this blessed life,' she writes.

Malika Booker (b. 1970 London) is the founder of the writers' collective 'Malika's Poetry Kitchen'. Her first collection, *Pepper Seed*, was shortlisted for the Seamus Heaney Centre Prize; she is a teaching fellow at the University of Leeds' creative writing department.

'The Little Miracles' takes as its point of departure Tomas Tranströmer's 'A Winter Night'; the raging storm of that poem is transformed into an interior storm, the poet's mother's stroke. Booker gives an uncompromising picture of the process of care and recovery – its fears, its effect on sibling relationships, its moments of false hope, its triumphs and gratitudes: 'each spoonful of pureed food slipped into her mouth / like a tender offering takes us a step away from feeding / tubes, and we are so thankful for each minuscule miracle'.

Regi Claire (b.1962 Münchwilen, Switzerland) has published two collections of short stories. '(Un)certainties' is not only her first published poem but the first poem she has written. An attempt to make sense of the death of her sister and her sister's partner in an accident at sea and the aftermath, it takes as its form a series of multiple-choice questions; although we are apparently offered a choice, the ambiguity in the title insinuates that there's little to choose between them.

Claire has described how she 'cried as I wrote "(Un)certainties", cried as I wrote and re-wrote, cried as I read aloud. But I couldn't let my sister go unsung.'

Valzhyna Mort (b. 1981 Minsk, Belarus, part of the former Soviet Union) moved to the United States in 2005 and teaches at Cornell University. 'Nocturne for a Moving Train' (set on a Belarusian night-train travelling from Minsk to Warsaw or Berlin) paints an unsettling portrait of an interior and exterior landscape: fugitive glimpses of places passed through, windows in which figures are seen to move 'as if performing surgery on tables'. Reflections multiply; signboards promise 'a possibility of words / for what flew by'; the landscape itself is on the edge of speech.

Mort has received the Crystal of Valencia Award, the Burda Prize for East European authors, and the Bess Hokin Prize from *Poetry* magazine (Chicago). Her third collection, *Music for the Dead and Resurrected* – which she has described as 'a book of letters to the dead' – is forthcoming from FSG.

Sarah Tsiang (b. 1978 Montreal, Canada) writes poems which deal uncompromisingly with contemporary sexual mores. 'Dick pics' is characteristically subversive and witty, with an eye for the unexpected image: 'a graffitied cock, standing on balls / pointing to the night sky, / like a fallen constellation'.

Tsiang was initially resistant to seeing herself as a poet: 'It seemed like a weighted, pretentious word and I wondered if I could still be a poet during my fallow times when I wasn't writing? Eventually I realized that the act of reading and writing poetry was enough – to be a poet is similar to other trades (though with less pay) in that much of it is putting your head down and getting to work.'

Publisher acknowledgements

Juana Adcock · The Guitar's Lament · *Split* · Blue Diode Publishing
Romalyn Ante · Kayumanggi · *Antiemetic for Homesickness* ·
   Chatto & Windus
Dean Atta · The Making · *Finished Creatures*
Sue Hyon Bae · After the Threesome, They Both Take You Home ·
   Truce Country · Eyewear Publishing
Fiona Benson · Mama Cockroach, I Love You · *Poetry London*
Tessa Berring · An Intention to Be Present · *Bitten Hair* ·
   Blue Diode Publishing
Caroline Bird · Dive Bar · Rookie · *The Air Year* · Carcanet
Malika Booker · The Little Miracles · *Magma*
Colette Bryce · A Last Post · *The M Pages* · Picador Poetry
Chen Chen · Year's End · *bath magg*
Eiléan Ní Chuilleanáin · Seaweed · *The Mother House* · The Gallery Press
Regi Claire · (Un)certainties · *Mslexia* and PBS Women's Poetry
   Competition
Jane Clarke · Copper Soles · *When the Tree Falls* · Bloodaxe Books
Natalie Diaz · Blood-Light · Waist and Sway · *Postcolonial Love Poem* ·
   Faber & Faber
Cath Drake · Our Front Garden · *The Shaking City* · Seren
Paul Farley · Quadrat · *The Mizzy* · Picador Poetry
Vicki Feaver · 1974 · The Larder · *I Want! I Want!* · Cape Poetry
Maria Ferguson · My Letters · *Alright, Girl?* · Burning Eye Books
Carolyn Forché · Museum of Stones · *In the Lateness of the World* ·
   Bloodaxe Books
Matthew Francis · Ladybird Summer · *Wing* · Faber & Faber
Ella Frears · Fucking in Cornwall · Sestina for Caroline Bergvall ·
   Shine, Darling · Offord Road Books
Mina Gorji · The Wasp · *Art of Escape* · Carcanet
Will Harris · My Name Is Dai · Yellow · *RENDANG* · Granta Poetry
Lesley Harrison · Thursday Poem · *Disappearance* · Shearsman Books
Michael Haslam · 16/2/47 · *Ickerbrow Trig* · Shearsman Books
Seán Hewitt · October · *Tongues of Fire* · Cape Poetry
Selima Hill · Thousands upon Thousands of Beetles · *I May Be Stupid
   But I'm Not That Stupid* · Bloodaxe Books

Katherine Horrex · Parliament, Fallen · *Growlery* · Carcanet

Avril Joy · Skomm · *Going in with flowers* · Linen Press

Peter Kahn · Little Kings · *Little Kings* · Nine Arches Press

Simon Lewis · Circle Time · *Ah, Men!* · Doire Press

Fran Lock · On insomnia · *Contains Mild Peril* · Out-Spoken Press

Rachel Long · The Omen · Red Hoover · *My Darling from the Lions* ·
    Picador Poetry

Ed Madden · A Pooka in Arkansas · *Poetry Bus Magazine*

Nick Makoha · They Will Call This Evidence · *SMOKE*

Rachel Mann · Book of Jonah · *A Kingdom of Love* · Carcanet

Mary McCollum · the boy with dark eyes · *living by the law of light* ·
    Dancing Sisters

Shane McCrae · The Hastily Assembled Angel on Care and Vitality ·
    Sometimes I Never Suffered · Corsair

Momtaza Mehri · Haematology #2 · Manchester Poetry Prize

Abegail Morley · Barometer · *The Unmapped Woman* · Nine Arches Press

David Morley · After the Burial of the Gypsy Matriarch · FURY ·
    FURY · Carcanet

Valzhyna Mort · Nocturne for a Moving Train · *The Poetry Review*

Paul Muldoon · Corncrake and Curlew · *Frolic and Detour* ·
    Faber & Faber

Sharon Olds · Departure Gate Aria · *Arias* · Cape Poetry

Roberto Pastore · Just So You Know · *Hey Bert* · Parthian Books

Don Paterson · Death · *Zonal* · Faber & Faber

Pascale Petit · Green Bee-eater · Tiger Gran · *Tiger Girl* ·
    Bloodaxe Books

David Pollard · 1543 · *Broken Voices* · Waterloo Press

Nina Mingya Powles · Conversational Chinese · Sonnet with particles
    of gold · *Magnolia, 木蘭* · Nine Arches Press

Michael Rosen · Raspberry Pip · *Mr Mensh* · Smokestack Books

Julie-ann Rowell · Fata Morgana · *Exposure* · Turas Press

Fiona Sampson · Mother as Eurydice · *Come Down* · Corsair

Tom Sastry · A man's house catches fire · *A Man's House Catches Fire* ·
    Nine Arches Press

Seni Seneviratne · Dear Dad · *Unknown Soldier* · Peepal Tree

Penelope Shuttle · Noah's Arche, Day One Hundred ·
    The Dark Horse

Winners of the Forward Prizes

Best Collection

2019 · Fiona Benson · *Vertigo & Ghost* · Cape Poetry

2018 · Danez Smith · *Don't Call Us Dead* · Chatto & Windus

2017 · Sinéad Morrissey · *On Balance* · Carcanet

2016 · Vahni Capildeo · *Measures of Expatriation* · Carcanet

2015 · Claudia Rankine · *Citizen: An American Lyric* · Penguin Books

2014 · Kei Miller · *The Cartographer Tries to Map a Way to Zion* · Carcanet

2013 · Michael Symmons Roberts · *Drysalter* · Cape Poetry

2012 · Jorie Graham · *PLACE* · Carcanet

2011 · John Burnside · *Black Cat Bone* · Cape Poetry

2010 · Seamus Heaney · *Human Chain* · Faber & Faber

2009 · Don Paterson · *Rain* · Faber & Faber

2008 · Mick Imlah · *The Lost Leader* · Faber & Faber

2007 · Sean O'Brien · *The Drowned Book* · Picador Poetry

2006 · Robin Robertson · *Swithering* · Picador Poetry

2005 · David Harsent · *Legion* · Faber & Faber

2004 · Kathleen Jamie · *The Tree House* · Picador Poetry

2003 · Ciaran Carson · *Breaking News* · The Gallery Press

2002 · Peter Porter · *Max is Missing* · Picador Poetry

2001 · Sean O'Brien · *Downriver* · Picador Poetry

2000 · Michael Donaghy · *Conjure* · Picador Poetry

1999 · Jo Shapcott · *My Life Asleep* · OUP

1998 · Ted Hughes · *Birthday Letters* · Faber & Faber

1997 · Jamie McKendrick · *The Marble Fly* · OUP

1996 · John Fuller · *Stones and Fires* · Chatto & Windus

1995 · Sean O'Brien · *Ghost Train* · OUP

1994 · Alan Jenkins · *Harm* · Chatto & Windus

1993 · Carol Ann Duffy · *Mean Time* · Anvil Press

1992 · Thom Gunn · *The Man with Night Sweats* · Faber & Faber

Best First Collection

2019 · Stephen Sexton · *If All the World and Love Were Young* · Penguin Books

2018 · Phoebe Power · *Shrines of Upper Austria* · Carcanet

2017 · Ocean Vuong · *Night Sky with Exit Wounds* · Cape Poetry

2016 · Tiphanie Yanique · *Wife* · Peepal Tree

2015 · Mona Arshi · *Small Hands* · Pavilion Poetry

2014 · Liz Berry · *Black Country* · Chatto & Windus

2013 · Emily Berry · *Dear Boy* · Faber & Faber

2012 · Sam Riviere · *81 Austerities* · Faber & Faber

2011 · Rachael Boast · *Sidereal* · Picador Poetry

2010 · Hilary Menos · *Berg* · Seren

2009 · Emma Jones · *The Striped World* · Faber & Faber

2008 · Kathryn Simmonds · *Sunday at the Skin Launderette* · Seren

2007 · Daljit Nagra · *Look We Have Coming to Dover!* · Faber & Faber

2006 · Tishani Doshi · *Countries of the Body* · Aark Arts

2005 · Helen Farish · *Intimates* · Cape Poetry

2004 · Leontia Flynn · *These Days* · Cape Poetry

2003 · AB Jackson · *Fire Stations* · Anvil Press

2002 · Tom French · *Touching the Bones* · The Gallery Press

2001 · John Stammers · *Panoramic Lounge-Bar* · Picador Poetry

2000 · Andrew Waterhouse · *In* · The Rialto

1999 · Nick Drake · *The Man in the White Suit* · Bloodaxe Books

1998 · Paul Farley · *The Boy from the Chemist is Here to See You* · Picador Poetry

1997 · Robin Robertson · *A Painted Field* · Picador Poetry

1996 · Kate Clanchy · *Slattern* · Chatto & Windus

1995 · Jane Duran · *Breathe Now, Breathe* · Enitharmon

1994 · Kwame Dawes · *Progeny of Air* · Peepal Tree

1993 · Don Paterson · *Nil Nil* · Faber & Faber

1992 · Simon Armitage · *Kid* · Faber & Faber

Best Single Poem

2019 · Parwana Fayyaz · Forty Names · *PN Review*

2018 · Liz Berry · The Republic of Motherhood · *Granta*

2017 · Ian Patterson · The Plenty of Nothing · *PN Review*

2016 · Sasha Dugdale · Joy · *PN Review*

2015 · Claire Harman · The Mighty Hudson · *Times Literary Supplement*

2014 · Stephen Santus · In a Restaurant · Bridport Prize

2013 · Nick MacKinnon · The Metric System · *The Warwick Review*

2012 · Denise Riley · A Part Song · *London Review of Books*

2011 · RF Langley · To a Nightingale · *London Review of Books*

2010 · Julia Copus · An Easy Passage · *Magma*

2009 · Robin Robertson · At Roane Head · *London Review of Books*

2008 · Don Paterson · Love Poem for Natalie "Tusja" Beridze ·
The Poetry Review

2007 · Alice Oswald · Dunt · *Poetry London*

2006 · Sean O'Brien · Fantasia on a Theme of James Wright ·
The Poetry Review

2005 · Paul Farley · Liverpool Disappears for a Billionth of a Second ·
The North

2004 · Daljit Nagra · Look We Have Coming to Dover! ·
The Poetry Review

2003 · Robert Minhinnick · The Fox in the Museum of Wales ·
Poetry London

2002 · Medbh McGuckian · She Is in the Past, She Has This Grace ·
The Shop

2001 · Ian Duhig · The Lammas Hireling · National Poetry Competition

2000 · Tessa Biddington · The Death of Descartes · Bridport Prize

1999 · Robert Minhinnick · Twenty-five Laments for Iraq · *PN Review*

1998 · Sheenagh Pugh · Envying Owen Beattie · *New Welsh Review*

1997 · Lavinia Greenlaw · A World Where News Travelled Slowly ·
Times Literary Supplement

1996 · Kathleen Jamie · The Graduates · *Times Literary Supplement*

1995 · Jenny Joseph · In Honour of Love · *The Rialto*

1994 · Iain Crichton Smith · Autumn · *PN Review*

1993 · Vicki Feaver · Judith · *Independent on Sunday*

1992 · Jackie Kay · Black Bottom · Bloodaxe Books

Supporting Poetry with Forward

The Forward Prizes for Poetry are a highlight of the literary year for poets, publishers and all who are committed to great contemporary writing. This year, with the booktrade disrupted, and live performances a distant memory, we need your help.

The Forward Arts Foundation is a charity that changes lives through poetry. We support poets, strengthen communities and give people the confidence to create & communicate, both through the Forward Prizes and through National Poetry Day. Become a supporter by contacting our Executive Director, susannah@forwardartsfoundation.org